BALI

First Edition, 2015
Updated, 2017
Lost Guides
www.thelostguides.com

Copyright
© Lost Guides, 2015

Author Anna Chittenden
Photographer Anna Chittenden
Editor Josie Ferguson
Designer Sarah and Schooling
Map Illustrator Lindsey Balbierz

Cover Image 'In Search of Salt' by
Pip Harwood seagypsea.com

Printed and bound in Singapore by Markono Print Media Pte Ltd

ISBN 978-981-09-7066-6

Work with Lost Guides
Lost Guides is able to deliver bespoke travel guides and custom
content for your business in both print and digital formats. If you like
what we do, please email *hello@thelostguides.com*

Stock this book
If you are interested in stocking *Lost Guides – Bali*, please email
hello@thelostguides.com

BALI

A UNIQUE, STYLISH AND OFFBEAT
TRAVEL GUIDE TO BALI

LOST GUIDES

1ST EDITION

ANNA CHITTENDEN

Contents

Author's Notes

Hello! I'm Anna, and I'm the author, photographer and explorer behind this book: *Lost Guides – Bali*. My love affair with Bali started a couple of years ago, and now I can't get enough of this wonderful island. To be honest, on my first visit here I didn't have a clue where to go and spent way too much time in the wrong places. However, I've now got to know Bali pretty well and have dug up all that is awesome to help you have an amazing trip!

Bali has something for everyone. Whether you're a fussy foodie, yoga bunny, serious surfer, culture vulture, art obsessive or you just want to relax to the max, this Indonesian island has it all.

What's in the guide?

The recommendations in this book are a highly curated selection of places that I know you'll love. I've personally visited each place and then tested the tips with like-minded travellers. Recommendations can range from secret beaches, boutique retreats and cool cafés to traditional artisans and surf spots. Designed to be practical and useful, this book is organised geographically from south to north, and into neighbourhoods, with maps and original photography to give you all the information that you need. I have also included the social media accounts of businesses so you can quickly see what they're up to in real time. This is by no means an exhaustive guide to Bali, more a selection of special spots to get you started on your journey.

How did I choose what would go in the book?

I'm naturally drawn to small and intimate places, where you might have the owner greeting you at the door, and you can feel their hard work and passion running through every aspect of the business. I love hearing a chef talk about their commitment to local sourcing or meeting an artist whose skills have been passed down through generations. I'm also very value conscious, so you'll see that I have recommended places that are affordable. Bali is a low-cost travel destination so there's no need to spend over the odds to stay somewhere lovely or to have a great meal.

Lastly, all the recommendations that appear in this book are here because they are great! I haven't accepted commissions or payments to feature places in this guide — in fact, most of the businesses have no idea that they're in it.

Who is this book for?

I have created this book for today's traveller - the stylish nomad with an interest in experience rather than expense and an eye for quality, design and authenticity. It is for those that don't require over-the-top luxury, nor have the budget of a backpacker — but are in search of those special places in-between.

About the Author

In 2014 I founded my travel website **www.thelostguides.com**, born out of the endless frustration of not finding useful and trustworthy information about where I wanted to travel. I now use this space to share unique and inspiring travel experiences in Asia and beyond, with the aim of helping to make your travel planning that little bit easier! Originally from the UK, I'm now based in Singapore where I run my website and work as a freelance travel writer for publications and companies, including *Condé Nast Traveller, The Business Times* and *Skyscanner. Lost Guides – Bali* is my first book.

Drop me a line

Your feedback is super important to me. I'd love to know your thoughts on the book, what you think could be improved, suggestions or any hidden gems you've uncovered on your travels. Please share your lovely photos of your trip with me using the hashtag **#lostguidesbali**

- ✉ anna@thelostguides.com
- ⓞ @lostguides
- 🐦 @lostguides
- 🅕 Lost Guides

Swing by **www.thelostguides.com** to see free online travel guides and to sign up to the newsletter.

Need to Know

Accommodation: Throughout this book you'll find a selection of my favourite places to stay. Luckily Bali has a huge amount of wonderful accommodation. It makes sense to book a villa as they are affordable, and you get more space and privacy than a hotel. Villas often have managers that can help with transport and transfers as well as housekeepers who will cook and clean, so you get the same benefits of a hotel too. I find *airbnb.com* the best way to find villas, and I also use *baliretreats.com.au* for unique accommodation.

Visas: Bali has recently updated its visa policy to allow free visa entry for the duration of 30 days for countries including the United Kingdom, Ireland, Singapore, United States, Australia, New Zealand, Netherlands, France, Germany, Italy, Japan, South Africa, Russia, Spain and many more. Please check with the Indonesian Embassy in your country for up-to-date visa information.

Money: The currency in Bali is Indonesian Rupiah – *Rp*. Be sure to get out cash in advance before you reach Bali, as the ATMs at the airport are often out of order. There are many ATMs on the island, but they limit the amount of cash that can be withdrawn at one time. Restaurants and hotels take cards, while cafés and smaller businesses often only take cash.

Transport: The roads in Bali are bad, so take extra care when driving or riding around the island. Your hotel or villa should help you with taxi transfers from the airport. Alternatively at the airport there is an 'airport taxi counter' as soon as you walk out of security. They are the official taxi providers and have a fixed price list for all destinations on the island. If you are in Seminyak, be sure to only use *Blue Bird* taxis and not their rogue imitators. Mopeds are a popular mode of transport and can be rented cheaply by the day. Car rental is also an affordable option. I must stress, however, how dangerous it can be to ride/drive around Bali, so consider taking a taxi or hiring a driver as an alternative option.

When to go: I might be biased, but I think that Bali is a great place to visit at any time of the year. It's fortunately one of those destinations where the weather can be good all year round. Peak season is July and August when families visit during the school holidays. I personally prefer to go outside these months, as otherwise I find the island too busy. November – April is officially wet season, although you can have days with bright blue skies. The tropical rains are heavy but brief.

Alcohol: Prices for most things in Bali are generally very reasonable. Beer is cheap, but watch out for the cost of wine and spirits, which can be similar to prices back home.

Note: in this book, where prices are listed as $ this is USD.

MT. BATUR

MT. AGUNG

UBUD

CANGGU

SEMINYAK

NUSA LEMBONGAN

BUKIT PENINSULA

Bukit Peninsula

Surfers' Spot and Bohemian Bolthole

Bukit Peninsula, or 'The Bukit' as it's known, has been a magnet for surfers since the '70s, who travelled from afar, drawn to the region's endless string of perfect Indo-waves. While nomadic surfers still descend on these shores in droves, the cliffside villages have now become a retreat for a new wave of bohemian traveller looking for a laid-back side to Bali. Located in the southernmost point of the island, The Bukit includes the hotspots **Uluwatu** – for die-hard surf fanatics, **Bingin** – with its beautiful beaches and boutique hideaways, **Balangan** – a quiet and simple surf spot, and **Jimbaran** – which has become more developed with high-end hotels but still maintains its traditional fish market.

The international crowd that come here aren't looking for smart city-style service; they are happy to spend their days perched on a surfboard, their evenings drinking Bintang beers at a ramshackled beach bar and their nights in a wooden Balinese bungalow on a cliff. For me this is what Bali is all about.

The Bukit is defined by its stunning shoreline with its craggy limestone cliffs, which tower over an azure-tinted ocean. The beaches here are how you'd imagine Bali's to be. Cream-coloured sand sweeps around the shoreline with piercing blue waters crashing on the coast. Steep cliff access means that the beaches are quiet aside from a sprinkling of cafés and local warungs. Don't miss a visit to this wonderful part of Bali – I might see you there.

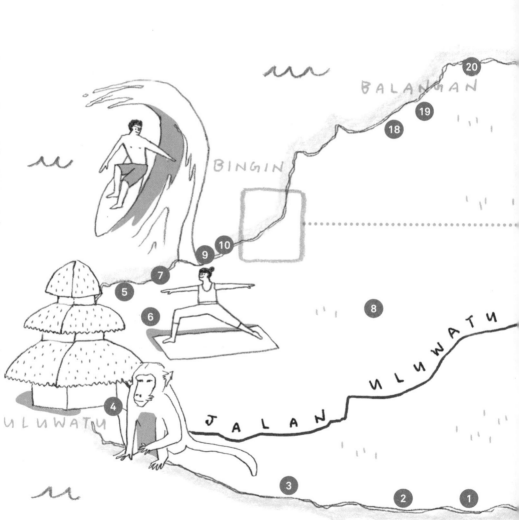

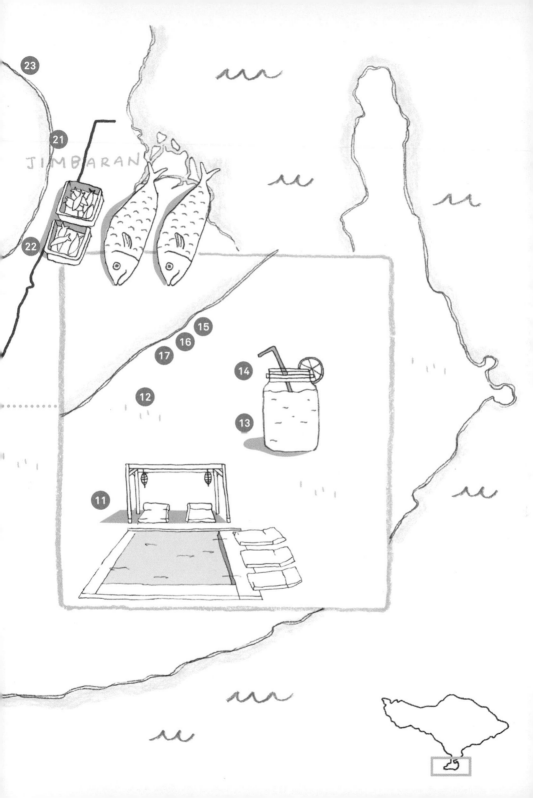

JIMBARAN

Sundays Beach Club

1 *Beautiful Beach Retreat*

It's safe to say that the south of Bali is home to many of the island's beach gems. While I'm happy enough to sip smoothies in the cafés on Bingin Beach, a trip to Sundays Beach Club is always a fun day out. With its rustic and relaxed Mediterranean vibe, Sundays hosts a private white sand beach with stunning turquoise-blue waters and an offshore coral reef. Located at The Ungasan resort, non-guests are also welcome and, for an entrance fee, have access to the beach club and can get involved in kayaking, snorkeling and stand-up paddle boarding. The food here is seriously tasty, ranging from grilled seafood to pizzas straight out of their stone oven. Come with a group of friends and settle in for the afternoon on the colourful beanbags with a glass of rosé in hand.

🏠 The Ungasan, Jalan Pantai Selatan Gau, Banjar Wijaya Kusum, Ungasan

☎ +62 8119421110

➤ sundaysbeachclub.com

📷 @sundaysbeachclub

🕐 8am – 10pm

💲 Entrance fee Rp 300k (adult), Rp 50k (child), which includes Rp150k restaurant credit and water sports equipment.

The Warung at Alila Uluwatu

2 *Indo Food with a View*

If you're in The Bukit and are looking for a more luxurious sort of lunch spot as well as some great Indonesian food, or perhaps like me you enjoy nosing around a swanky hotel, then *The Warung* at *Alila Villas Uluwatu* is the place to go. *The Warung* offers traditional Indonesian cuisine with a modern twist, not to mention to-die-for views. The food is done by region, so you can experience the tastes of Java, Bali and Sumatra all in one meal. The chicken and beef satays are a must, as is the 'hasil laut panggang' – Balinese grilled seafood with lobster, squid, fish and prawns. Finish off your meal with homemade ice cream, 'es krim dadar', with a coconut pancake. Their wine list is good too, which is handy to know as it can be hard to find decent wine down in this area.

🏠 Jalan Belimbing Sari, Banjar Tambiyak, Desa Pecatu

☎ +62 3618482166

🔍 alilahotels.com/uluwatu

📷 @alilavillasuluwatu

🕐 11am – 11pm

Nyang Nyang Beach

(3) *Paradise Lost*

When I hear people say that Bali doesn't have any good beaches, I smile to myself and think of Nyang Nyang. You often read about 'secret beaches', which aren't actually that secret anymore. Nyang Nyang Beach, on the other hand, has managed to keep its location and identity firmly on the down-low. One reason is that it's pretty hard to find (read dirt track, fields and 500 cliffside steps). Once you get there, however, you'll be rewarded with your own little bit of paradise all to yourself. The last time I visited Nyang Nyang there was no one else there other than a few local children spearfishing in the sea. And by deserted, I mean really deserted, i.e. no drinks stalls, umbrellas or food – so bring your own supplies and shade. Good luck on your mission!

Getting There
Best done on a bike. Head towards Uluwatu Temple. You can go right towards the temple, or left – go left, past *Ulu Café*. Carry on another 100m until you see two white pillars just before some warungs and a launderette. Turn right down the thin pavement until the road ends. You should see a small wooden sign saying 'Nyang Nyang surf beach'. Follow the dirt track until it becomes a field with a few ruins. Walk to the end of the cliff where you will find a small drinks stall (stock up!). Make your way down the 500 steps to the beach. Enjoy!

Uluwatu Temple

4 *Spiritual Cliffside Stunner*

$ Rp50k entrance fee

Slightly south of the surf breaks at Uluwatu Beach lies the Hindu temple known locally as Pura Luhur Uluwatu. The draw here isn't so much the structure itself (Bali has more impressive temples dotted around the island), but the striking scenery. Situated on a limestone cliff 70m above the roaring ocean, it is especially beautiful at sunset. One of the oldest in Bali, this sacred sea temple was originally built in the 11th century and has links to other sea temples, such as Tanah Lot in West Bali. As this is a place of worship, make sure to cover up with appropriate clothes (they have sarongs available to borrow at the entrance). Also be aware of your belongings, as although they are said to be the protectors of the temple, there are teams of mischievous monkeys ready to snatch your bag.

Uluwatu Beach and Suluban Beach

5 *Hidden Beaches at a Surfers' Paradise*

Uluwatu Beach might be one of the smallest on the island, but it could also be one of the most beautiful. With dramatic rock formations, caves and big crashing waves from the surf break, it's worth the walk down the steep cliff to check this little place out. The beach is mainly used by experienced surfers who want to reach the famous Uluwatu surf spot (Kelly Slater calls it one of the seven wonders of surf). While there isn't much opportunity for sunbathing (you're in a cave!), I like to go up to the café *Delphi Warung* to get the best views of the Indian Ocean while watching the surfers in action. Neighbouring Uluwatu is the swimmer-friendly Suluban Beach with stunning turquoise waters. If you're planning a visit you'll need to get your timings right though, as it's only accessible at low tide.

Getting There
When you reach the village of Uluwatu, park up and you will see cafés and bars, such as *Single Fin* at the top of the cliff. Walk down the steps until you get to Uluwatu Beach. Suluban Beach is just to the left of Uluwatu Beach.

Morning Light Yoga

6 *Ocean and Jungle View Zen*

After a morning of being battered about by waves, there's nothing better than coming to this breezy open-air yoga studio to stretch out those surf pains. Surrounded by lush foliage and situated high enough to enjoy views of the ocean, this traditional wooden-thatched hut is blissfully serene. Drop-in classes teaching Vinyasa Flow are held every day at 7.30am, 10.30am and 5.30pm and are open to all levels of experience: just arrive a few minutes before the class starts. I, for one, find the sessions particularly challenging, but they do give you a great workout and you'll see improvements after a few days. You'll find the studio located in the peaceful grounds of the lovely *Uluwatu Surf Villas*.

🏠 Uluwatu Surf Villas, Jalan Pantai Suluban, Uluwatu

☎ +62 817555421

↖ uluwatusurfvillas.com/yoga

f Morning Light Yoga Bali

📷 @morninglightyoga

⏱ 7.30am, 10.30am and 5.30pm daily

$ Rp100k per class

Single Fin

7 *Surfers' Sunset Beach Bar*

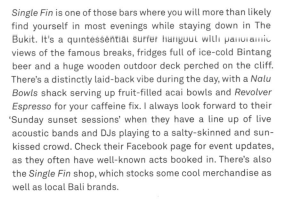

Single Fin is one of those bars where you will more than likely find yourself in most evenings while staying down in The Bukit. It's a quintessential surfer hangout with panoramic views of the famous breaks, fridges full of ice-cold Bintang beer and a huge wooden outdoor deck perched on the cliff. There's a distinctly laid-back vibe during the day, with a *Nalu Bowls* shack serving up fruit-filled acai bowls and *Revolver Espresso* for your caffeine fix. I always look forward to their 'Sunday sunset sessions' when they have a line up of live acoustic bands and DJs playing to a salty-skinned and sun-kissed crowd. Check their Facebook page for event updates, as they often have well-known acts booked in. There's also the *Single Fin* shop, which stocks some cool merchandise as well as local Bali brands.

🏠 Blue Point, Uluwatu

📞 +62 361769941

➤ singlefinbali.com

📘 Single Fin – Bali

📷 @singlefin_bali

🕐 Mon, Tues, Thurs, Fri and Sat
11am – 10pm, Wed 11am-12am,
Sun 11am – 1am

Sunset Paradise Villa

8 *Luxurious Party Pad*

If you come to Bali with a group of friends, it becomes amazingly affordable to rent one of the many beautiful villas on the island. This eight-person pad will only set you back $45 per person per night. The bedrooms come with en-suite bathrooms and there's a two-tiered swimming pool – lush! I love the mix of 20th century Javanese architecture in the living area matched with the contemporary design found throughout the rest of the villa. There is on-site staff on hand to help with anything from booking a taxi to arranging an in-villa massage. They can also organise a private chef to cook a BBQ dinner for you with seafood from nearby Jimbaran Bay. The location of the villa is slightly out of the way, but what you do get is a little bit of luxury for a small price.

↖ airbnb.com/rooms/4026549

$ $366 per night

Padang Padang Beach

9 *Sand, Swim and Surf*

A quiet and secluded beach ten minutes north from rough and ready Uluwatu Beach, Padang Padang is the perfect place to relax and take in the glorious Bukit coastline. I suggest coming here early in the morning for a swim when you can enjoy this stunning bit of sand and sea all to yourself. Not all beaches in Bali are suitable for swimming so this is a great spot. Padang Padang is also a good place to learn to surf, compared to somewhere like Kuta, which is packed with surf schools. There are plenty of local teachers around, or you can hire a board from the beach if you've already got some surf skills. On Padang Padang Beach you'll find simple warungs serving nasi goreng and refreshing drinks, and look out for the colourful boat yard where they dismantle the fishing boats every time they take them out of the sea.

Getting There

Look out for places such as *Pinkcoco Bali Hotel* and the *ilovebali* clothes shop – you are in Padang Padang. Carry on until you see signs for the beach. There are normally lots of motorbikes parked at the top. Note: you will need to walk down some steep steps to get down to the beach.

Le Sabot

10 *Surf-In Surf-Out Cliffside Shacks*

🏹 lesabotbali.com

✉ padang@lesabotbali.com

$ From $57 per room per night
incl. breakfast

This place isn't for everyone, but if, like me, you're a fan of the simple life then *Le Sabot* might be right up your street. These eco-friendly, thatched bamboo huts are built into the cliff and are just a couple of metres from the roaring ocean. This little place was dreamt up by a sprightly Belgian guy called Eric, who moved to Bali to live out his dream of sleeping by the beach and surfing every day. I suggest you make good friends with Eric – if you're lucky he'll divulge some of his secret island hotspots with you. The four simple rooms all have ocean views, and you only need to roll out of bed and you are in the sea for a day of surfing at nearby Padang Padang. The showers are hot, and a friendly Balinese family is on hand to make you omelettes and coffee for breakfast.

Sal Secret Spot

11 *Whitewashed Wonderland*

The most HEAVENLY hideaway. It was tempting to abide by its namesake and keep this place a secret, but it's just too good not to share. Set up by a Portuguese guy who moved to Bali for the surf (don't they all!), *Sal* is affordable and intimate with only ten rooms. With whitewashed walls, outdoor bathrooms and a perfect pool, it feels like a Mediterranean retreat set up in the village of Bingin. You can choose between a cliffside room with panoramic views over the Bukit surf, or a bungalow by the pool. For breakfast they put on a spread of fresh fruit and cooked eggs, and for afternoon poolside lounging you can order jugs of Sangria. There's a cabana for massages and large Balinese day beds can be found dotted around under palm trees (the perfect place to leaf through your book). This has to be one of my favourite places to stay in Bali, and I've sent so many people here who all agree that it's just the dream.

🏠 Jalan Pantai Bingin

☎ +62 81238942686

↖ salbalihotel.com

✉ sal.bungalows@outlook.com

💲 From $65 per room per night
incl. breakfast

The Temple Lodge

(12) *Bohemian Surf and Yoga Retreat*

High above the cliffs of Bingin is the super-chic surf and yoga retreat *The Temple Lodge*. Seven suites have been lovingly designed using local natural materials with colourful carved wood and traditional thatched roofs. The rooms are open air in style, so you can feel truly at one with nature while falling asleep to the sound of the waves crashing below. Geared towards a healthy lifestyle, there are daily yoga classes, a vegetarian menu and the spoiling *Temple Spa*. The 'Temple Suite' has its own private swimming pool and huge living space, while the other rooms share a lovely cliffside infinity pool. Spend your days relaxing at the retreat or head down to the beach at Bingin for a swim, sunbathe and surf session. Non-guests can also enjoy the yoga studio or book in for a meal at the restaurant.

🏠 Jalan Pantai Bingin

☎ +62 85739011572

↖ thetemplelodge.com

✉ thetemplelodge@outlook.com

$ From $70 per room per night incl. breakfast

The Cashew Tree

13 *Organic Café with Live Music*

Located up in Bingin village, *The Cashew Tree* is a casual café in a relaxing garden with lazy loungers, beanbags and wooden cabanas. They pride themselves on using as many organic and local products as possible, serving up super healthy meals, such as pumpkin tofu cashew curry, spicy Asian chicken salad and my favourite: the raw cacao dessert. The café is conveniently situated within walking distance from most of Bingin's accommodation, so you'll probably end up popping in at least once a day to pick up a cleansing cucumber juice, coffee or curry. Be sure to stick around for their weekly 'Thursday Sessions' when live bands play, and pretty much everyone in the village attends to dance the night away.

🏠 Jalan Pantai Bingin

📘 The Cashew Tree

📷 thecashewtree

🕐 10am – 10pm

Acacia Bungalows

14 *Spacious and Serene Hideaway*

If you want slightly more space and privacy compared to the other Bingin boutique hotels mentioned, then look no further than *Acacia Bungalows*. Managed by the same people as *Mick's Place*, *Acacia* is similar in style, but each of its bungalows also benefit from having their own private entrance, garden and swimming pool. Staff are discreetly on hand to make you breakfast and to help with anything you need — be it a taxi, a restaurant recommendation, surf lessons or a spa booking. As well as the private pool, my favourite part is the huge outdoor bathrooms where you can indulge in an open air shower under a canopy of pink bougainvillea flowers. Spa treatments and massages can be arranged at the bungalow, so you can have a pedicure whist reading on a sun lounger next to the pool — spoiling!

🏠 Jalan Pantai Bingin

☎ +61 755363325

↖ baliretreats.com.au/acacia

✉ info@baliretreats.com.au

$ From $107 per room per night incl. breakfast

Mick's Place

15 *Breathtaking Boutique Bolthole*

Who needs a big, brash, soulless hotel when you can stay at this charming cliffside hideaway? *Mick's Place* is my favourite type of accommodation – 'laid-back luxury' featuring wooden tree houses and Polynesian-style bungalows. The wow factor is the location; *Mick's Place* is uniquely situated right on top of the cliff looking down over the surf at Bingin Beach. There's a small infinity plunge pool, the perfect place to chill out with a cocktail, and be sure to book yourself in for a massage at the 'spa with a view'. The best room is the 'Honeymoon Bungalow', which has its own private pool, garden, daybeds and an indoor-outdoor bathroom – ideal for a romantic escape. Also a popular place for weddings, check out their insta @micksplacebali for the dreamiest 'take me here now' photos. Note, *Mick's Place* is adults-only, taking guests over 12 years old.

🏠 Jalan Pantai Bingin

☎ +61 755363325

↖ baliretreats.com.au/micksplace

✉ info@baliretreats.com.au

📷 @micksplacebali

💲 From $94 per room per night incl. breakfast

Kelly's Warung

16 *Barefoot Beach Shack*

Located right on Bingin Beach, *Kelly's* is the go-to place for a post-yoga or post-surf refuel. Run by the same crew as *The Cashew Tree*, the menu is healthy but hearty, serving up pink pitaya fruit bowls, raw vegetable wraps and refreshing juices. Grab a seat on the wooden deck at *Kelly's* for wonderful panoramic views over the beach, and watch the surfers at play in the ocean in front of you. The vibe is super friendly so you'll probably end up making a few new pals while you're here. Surfers from Brazil, families from Norway, locals from Uluwatu — it's a lovely mix of people who all appreciate the simple things in life. *Kelly's* also provides cheap and cheerful accommodation above the café: perfect for beach bums who like to roll straight out of bed and onto the sand.

 Bingin Beach

 Kellys Warung

 @kellyswarung

Bingin Beach

 Beautiful Bukit Beach

This has to be one of my favourite beaches in Bali. Not only because it has soft white sand, crystal turquoise waters and a lack of crowds, but also because Bingin is one of those friendly, unpretentious places where travellers come and chat over dragon fruit smoothies at *Kelly's Warung*, or trade travel secrets while sitting on their surf boards waiting for a wave. The beach is at the bottom of a steep limestone cliff, which you access via stone steps. There are dozens of wooden thatched huts and a few simple villas to rent, all with amazing ocean views. As well as being a good swimming spot, Bingin is a lovely place to come for a surf and is suitable for all ranges of experience. If, like me, you prefer to go with a guide, there are lots of teachers located at the beach who can take you out for a morning surf. Come evening, Bingin Beach hosts seafood BBQs and bonfires. Bliss!

Getting There
Make your way to Bingin village. Once there, follow signs to the beach.
Note: the beach is about a seven-minute walk down some steep steps.

Balangan Beach

18 *Simple and Unspoilt Beach*

This coastal stretch has long been a favourite with surfers drawn to its reef break, but for those looking for a laid-back beach day, Balangan should also be top of your list. Somehow this beautiful, palm-fringed gem has managed to stay under the radar. Host to only a handful of local warungs in wooden shacks serving up snacks of nasi goreng and Bintang beer, it makes a change to the international beach-club scene of Seminyak. Swimmers can enjoy the waters when the sea is at high tide, and for those that want to laze around, the beach is lined with sun loungers and umbrellas, which can be rented for Rp50k for the day. It's worth a trip to Balangan just to see its breathtaking scenery, which is especially magical at sunset.

Getting There
Balangan Beach is easily accessible compared to the other cliffside beaches of The Bukit. Drive to Balangan village, and leave your car or bike in the car park. It's a short walk from there.

La Joya II Biu - Biu

19 *Stunning and Stylish Sanctuary*

Rustic and charming, this place really has to be seen to be believed. Located up from Balangan Beach, *La Joya II Biu-Biu* is a tiny village of eco-friendly bungalows set high up on a cliff looking out over the blue Indian Ocean. The accommodation is simple but comfortable; the buildings are made from locally found limestone and wood, and they have traditional thatched roofs. The wow factor comes from the curved, turquoise infinity pool with stunning panoramic views over the Bukit coastline. An experience not to be missed is treating yourself to a Balinese massage at their open-air 'Sel-Spa', a sort of spa in the clouds elevated just above the cliff's edge. Book yourself to stay in the 'Sel Hut', a quirky loft-like villa with its own private plunge pool and sun lounging area.

🏠 Jalan Pantai Balangan

☎ +62 8113990048

🡅 la-joya.com

✉ informations@la-joya.com

$ From $73 per night

Rock Bar

 Cliffside Cocktails

You will find *Rock Bar* at the top of many 'bars with the best view' lists, and it's not hard to see why. Reached via a near-vertical inclinator, this bar is literally built into the rock with 360-degree views and waves crashing right in front of you. Open just in the evening, it's part of the rather busy *Ayana Resort*, with non-guests welcome from 4pm. This isn't a quiet spot; expect it to be bustling with people come sunset. It's a lively and fun atmosphere with resident DJs playing on a platform set in the cliff-face and a long drinks menu with signature cocktails like 'Rock My World' and the dangerous sounding 'Bartender's Rock Shots' – comprising of six of the bartender's shots of the day.

 Ayana Resort & Spa, Jimbaran

 +62 361702222

 ayanaresort.com/rockbarbali

 rockbar@ayanaresort.com

 @rockbarbali

 Mon – Thurs 4pm – 1am
Fri – Sun 4pm – 2am

Cuca

21 *Innovative Cocktails and Culinary Creations*

🏠 Jalan Yoga Perkanthi,
Jimbaran

☎ +62 361708066

🔦 cucaflavor.com

✉ service@cucaflavor.com

📘 Cuca

📷 @cucaflavor

I first heard whispers of *Cuca* from a mixologist at one of my favourite bars in Singapore; word of mouth recommendations from industry insiders often lead me to the best finds. Head Chef Kevin Cherkas picked up his trade from working at Michelin-starred restaurants, such as *El Bulli* in Spain, and he now runs this fab dining venue with his wife Virginia in the coconut groves of Jimbaran. Start your evening off at their alfresco bar; the cocktails are creations in themselves – think fruity alcoholic ice-lollies balanced artfully on glasses. The food is tapas-style sharing dishes divided into three categories: 'harvested' – vegetables, 'hooked' – seafood, and 'farmed' – meat. The small plates mean that you have a good excuse to order whatever you like off the menu. Just don't get too full for dessert.

Jimbaran Fish Market

22 *Barefoot Beachside Dining*

Jimbaran Bay has traditionally been a fishing village where many of Bali's restaurants come to get their supplies. While the area now features many large resorts, there's still a distinctly local feel on the beach where you'll find clusters of colourful wooden fishing boats and fishermen hauling in their catch of the day. If you come in the morning you can visit the bustling wet market, where locals set up stands selling their produce. Around sunset, the beach glows with romantic candle-lit tables while diners select from the day's fresh catch, such as live crab, lobster and fish, to be grilled for their dinner. Enjoy the sea breeze, bury your feet in the sand and eat like a king. The prices are reasonable too.

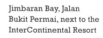 Jimbaran Bay, Jalan
Bukit Permai, next to the
InterContinental Resort

Jimbaran Market

23 *Lively Local Hangout*

This can hardly be considered a proper market, but what it lacks in size it makes up for in colour and charm. You will see women selling their wares and bright, fragrant flowers scattered all over the roadside. Baskets of green limes, beans and courgettes line the pavement, and laughing ladies gossip over shiny, red apples and light blue hydrangeas. I'm personally fascinated with the beautiful offerings nestled in palm leaf baskets, known as 'canang sari'. The Balinese people laboriously assemble these each morning from petals, and you can see them being made here. Even though it's near the tourist hotspots, it's nice to see a more local side to Bali that's often hidden. Pop by for a quick stop on your way to *Jimbaran fish market* and pick up a handful of fruit for your journey.

 Find this market towards the northern part of Jimbaran Bay, on Jalan Pantai Kedonganan.

Seminyak

Stylish Shopping and Fabulous Food

Known as the most happening place in Bali, Seminyak has grown up from being a small village populated by the island's expats, to one of the most stylish spots in South East Asia. Set against a soft sandy beach with tall crashing waves, Seminyak is a unique town heavily influenced by the Australian and European inhabitants who have made Bali their home. The vibe is totally international – you'll find a French restaurant opposite an Argentinian BBQ warehouse, all against the backdrop of peaceful paddy fields under Bali's bright blue skies.

One of the most exciting sides to Seminyak is the food. World-class chefs who've tired of city life have hopped over to the shores of Bali, enticed by the beach lifestyle as well as the fantastic local produce. Enjoy innovative Asian food with a twist or fancy European fare without the hefty price tag. If you're looking for a party, you'll find boisterous beach clubs and bustling bars dotted all around town.

If you want to stock up your summer wardrobe, you have come to the right place. The shopping in Seminyak is superb. You've got designers from across the globe working with talented Balinese artisans to produce high quality clothing and accessories, many of which are handmade, at affordable prices.

It must be noted that as the town has become more developed, the streets are busy and the traffic is heavy. I personally prefer to stay outside of Seminyak so as to get some down time away from the hustle and bustle. I normally find a quiet villa around neighbouring Canggu – a short 15-minute drive away.

SEMINYAK

5

16

22

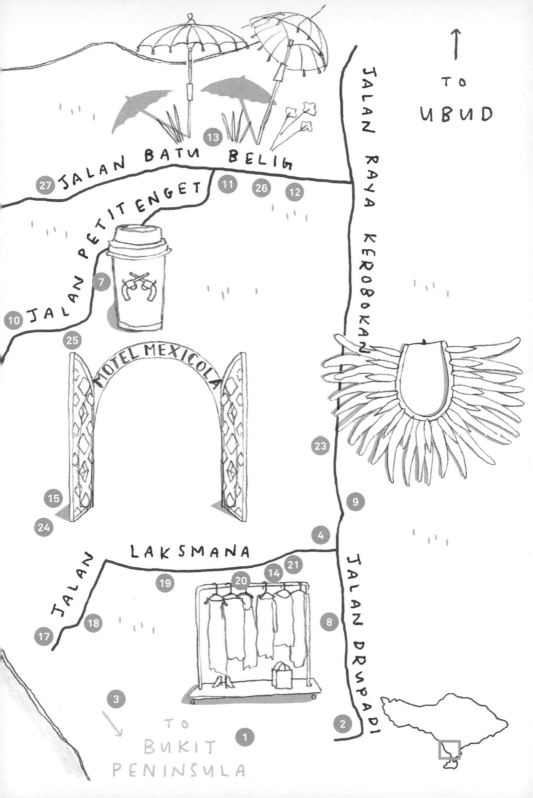

Kreol Kitchen

① *Homely Soul Café*

Tucked away on a quiet back road is the most delightful all-day café, *Kreol Kitchen*. The Aussie owner, Annick, has created a casual and calm space overlooking a rice paddy field, providing what she describes as 'soul food cooked with passion'. Pots of tea come with floral vintage cups, the menus are wrapped in second-hand children's storybooks and the homemade food, such as omelettes, pies, mezze and salads, are as plentiful as they are delicious. With jazz music playing softly in the background and feathered dream catchers swaying in the wind, Annick has created an environment infused with positive energy. In keeping with the café's spiritual vibe, she also sidelines as an intuitive Tarot card reader – just message the *Kreol Kitchen* Facebook page to book yourself an appointment.

🏠 Jalan Drupadi, 56

☎ +62 361738514

↖ kreolkitchen.com

f Kreol Kitchen

📷 @kreolkitchen

⊘ Mon – Sat 8am – 10pm

Nalu Bowls

2 *Fruity Surfers' Breakfasts*

🏠 Jalan Drupadi, 1 2A

☎ +62 81236609776

↖ nalubowls.com

🅕 Nalu Bowls

📷 @nalubowls

🕖 7.30am – 6pm

Taking inspiration from Hawaii where acai bowls are all the rage, *Nalu* (meaning 'wave' in Hawaiian) was set up to fill that smoothie-shaped hole in Seminyak's snack scene. What looks like nothing more than a whitewashed shack made of driftwood, *Nalu Bowls* cheerfully churns out stacks of coconut shells filled with blended fruit to happy and hippie customers. Each bowl is lovingly named after the owners' favourite waves from around the world. My go-to flavour is the 'Uluwatu' – filled with dragon fruit, banana, mango and raspberry. Hidden away down a narrow road off Jalan Seminyak, this place is sought out by those in the know and is best reached by bike with a surfboard in tow. They also have sister sites at *Single Fin* down in Uluwatu and at Echo Beach in Canggu catering to the hungry surfers.

The Straw Hut

(3) *Hidden Poolside Haven*

Drive for five minutes down the bumpy road next to *The Oberoi* hotel and you will find the hidden oasis that is *The Straw Hut*. One of Seminyak's only cafés with a pool, this is a lovely place to come and chill out whilst feasting on organic food and fresh-pressed juices. The food ranges from healthy dishes such as watermelon and avocado salad, to local inspired meals like Balinese crispy duck, to your popular pizza and pasta plates. This is a delightful café to come to during the day. Bring your holiday novel, sun hat and towel, and settle in on a beanbag, while sipping on smoothies, in between cooling off in the swimming pool. While the daytime is calm, *The Straw Hut* is known for their Friday night parties where live bands and DJs play to a youthful crowd.

🏠 Jalan Sari Dewi, 17

☎ +62 361736750

↖ thestrawhut.com

f The Straw Hut

📷 @thestrawhut

🕐 7.30am – 11pm

Corner House

4 *Airy Aussie Brunch Spot*

🏠 Jalan Laksmana, 10A

☎ +62 361730276

✉ info@cornerhousebali.com

📷 @cornerhousebali

🕐 7am – 12am

When you combine the creativity of a French fashion designer with an Australian photographer and put it into a restaurant, it looks something a bit like *Corner House*. Located in a light and lofty warehouse-style building, the interiors are distinctly European, while the menu is slightly more Melbourne. Sit yourself down at a country farmhouse table and order up a brunch of eggs benedict, pancakes with maple syrup or a hearty Angus beef burger. Conveniently situated on the same road as all the best boutiques, *Corner House* is a great place for a mid-shop pit stop. Open all day, the vibe of the restaurant is warm and welcoming with a charming courtyard providing the perfect place for chats over morning coffees.

Watercress

5 *Fresh, Organic Breakfasts*

With a focus on fresh, seasonal ingredients and inspiring flavours, this quiet and casual café has become a firm favourite with those looking for a healthy food fill. I like coming here for what they call their 'rustic breakfast', with options such as 'salmon & the rye', with avocado, pesto and cream cheese, or the 'Watercress omelette', with organic asparagus and zesty lemon crème fraîche. It's not all strictly healthy though, *Watercress* brings in freshly made cakes and croissants from bakery *Monsieur Spoon*, and you can get your caffeine fix here from Bali's own *Revolver Espresso*. They're also open for dinner, when you can tuck into cheese and charcuterie plates, French wine and piña colada cocktails. Useful to note is that *Watercress* has parking facilities, unlike many of the cafés and restaurants in central Seminyak.

🏠 Jalan Batu Belig, 21a

☎ +62 85102808030

🔦 watercressbali.com

✉ info@watercressbali.com

📘 Watercress cafe

📷 @watercressbali

🕐 Mon – Sat 7.30am – 4pm and
6pm – 12am, Sun 7.30am – 5pm

La Lucciola

6 *Breezy Beachfront Dining*

One of Seminyak's few beachside lunch locations (not including the restaurants in resorts), the Italian inspired *La Lucciola* has been around for a while and is a popular pick with returning visitors to the island. This is seaside dining like it should be: palm trees swaying in the wind, waves lapping on the shore and a stretch of golden sandy beach right in front of the restaurant. Housed in an open-air structure with a thatched roof and bamboo chairs, there's a cool ocean breeze that circulates around the building. The service is excellent, the staff super friendly and the prices are surprisingly reasonable. They're known for their tasty Italian pastas as well as fresh fish and the most refreshing fruit juices. *La Lucciola* is more of a daytime eating spot (due to its view), although it's also lovely for a cocktail or two come sunset.

🏠 Jalan Petitenget (next to Petitenget Temple)

☎ +62 361730838

🕐 9am – 11pm

Baby Revolver

(7) *Hip Coffee Hideaway*

While a *Starbucks* cup was a fashion accessory for New Yorkers in the noughties, a *Revolver* cup isn't far off this for a Seminyak scenester worth their salt. The younger sister of the popular *Revolver Espresso* near Seminyak Square, '*Baby Revs*' is a little hole in the wall boutique coffee house providing a haven for hipster caffeine lovers. With only eight seats, the retro styled interior is pretty cosy, but its location up on quiet Jalan Petitenget means that you'll normally find a space to squeeze in. Coffee geeks will love the fact that *Baby Revolver* uses La Marzocco coffee machines and Mazzer grinders, and layabouts will love that they do delivery to your hotel or villa. *Revolver Espresso* is considered by many to be the best coffee in Bali, and you'll see it being served at other hip hangouts like *Single Fin* and *Corner House*.

🏠 Jalan Petitenget, 102

☎ +62 85102444468

🖱 revolverespresso.com

✉ info@revolverespresso.com

📘 Revolver Espresso

📷 @revolverespresso

🕐 7am – 6pm

Kilo

8 *Laid-back Lounge*

🏠 Jalan Drupadi, 22

☎ +62 3614741006

↖ kilokitchen.com/bali

✉ bali@kilokitchen.com

📷 @kilobali

🕐 5.30pm – 12am

After establishing itself as a local favourite in Singapore, the cool and casual restaurant *Kilo* has hopped over the shores and landed in this delightfully-designed minimalist building sitting discreetly along Jalan Drupadi. The vibe is very Californian; think industrial meets desert with bold concrete walls and cactuses strewn on colourful Aztec carpets. The *Kilo* concept encourages its guests to share, which is great as you'll have a hard time choosing between delicious dishes such as wasabi tuna tartare, salt baked snapper and the 24-hour pork belly. With an emphasis on using local ingredients, the menu is presented under 'Raw', 'Warm', 'Comfort', 'Green' and 'Sweets'. And don't forget to try their bespoke cocktails for the full *Kilo* experience – my personal preference being 'A Sure Thing': homemade vanilla-infused vodka served with cucumber, mint and lime.

Mama San

(9) *Stylish Asian Street Food*

For those of you that have had the pleasure of travelling and eating your way around Asia, you will know that the heart of any Asian country's food scene lies in its street food. Chef Will Meyrick brings a new twist to the Bali restaurant line up by serving innovative and fun dishes inspired by his travels, such as Vietnamese pork belly, crispy salmon with green mango, Thai beef salad and Bagan chicken curry. Set in a trendy former 'gudang', or warehouse, the design of the restaurant has a feel of a 1920's colonial gentlemen's club, with marble top mah-jong tables and oversized tan leather chesterfields. A handy tip to know is that, while the main dining room downstairs is often pre-booked, you can turn up and eat upstairs in the comfy cocktail lounge where reservations aren't required.

Jalan Raya Kerobokan, 135

+62 361730436

mamasanbali.com

info@mamasanbali.com

MamaSan Bali

@mamasanbali

12pm – 3pm and
6.30pm – 11pm

Merah Putih

(10) *Fantastic Indonesian Fare*

If I land in Bali and can get out of the airport in time for dinner, I'll often race to Merah Putih for that first taste of Indonesian cuisine. Begin your evening at their snazzy bar and order a refreshing cucumber and mint martini. If you are with a group of friends, book a table in one of the cosy teak pods on the mezzanine, looking over the beautifully designed restaurant. The food on the menu, split into 'traditional' and 'modern', is a great way to understand more about the local cuisine from Bali as well as other Indo islands. It's hard to pick the best dish, but for starters I like the Bakwan Kepiting (soft-shell crab fritter), the Javanese beef shank steamed buns, and the coconut smoked yellowfin tuna. For mains go for the Balinese beef cheek curry and roast pork belly, as well as lots of sides like gado gado and sambal.

🏠 Jalan Petitenget, 100x

☎ +62 3618465950

↖ merahputihbali.com

f Merah Putih Bali

📷 @merahputihbali

🕐 12pm – 3pm, 8pm – 11pm

Métis

11 *Fancy French Food*

Set against the stunning backdrop of lush rice fields and a large lily pond, *Métis* is one of those places you come to if you want a truly romantic evening. The food here is Mediterranean inspired with an added dose of Balinese hospitality. For starters I'd go for the 'Trio Tartare', consisting of tuna with wasabi, crab and salmon, or, if you want to go full French, order 'Les Escargots'! The seafood here is marvelous, as is their meat selection – try their slow cooked lamb shank. Do leave space for dessert; it's one of their fortes. It's hard to resist the salted butter and caramel millefeuille. The standard of wine is what you'd expect from a restaurant headed up by a French chef, although like many of the higher end restaurants in Bali, it can get pricey if you get carried away.

Jalan Petitenget, 6

+62 3614737888

metisbali.com

info@metisbali.com

Metis Restaurant & Gallery Bali

@metis_bali

Mon – Sat 11am – 2am
Sun 6pm – 2am

Barbacoa

(12) *Smokey South American Grill*

When you walk into this rustic warehouse, the first thing you'll notice is the huge open fire stacked with logs, slowly barbecuing a whole pig. You can safely say that this isn't the best place for vegetarians. Taking inspiration for its food from South America, *Barbacoa* brings the asado-style atmosphere of an Argentinian social gathering to Bali. The tapas type dishes encourage you to try a big portion of their menu, from Cuban pulled pork sliders, Peruvian snapper ceviche to the more meaty charcoal-grilled beef rib eye. If you come for lunch you can sit out on the terrace overlooking the lovely rice paddy fields. For dinner, get stuck into their cocktail menu. I recommend the 'Silent Assassin' with chilli vodka, raspberry and coriander root.

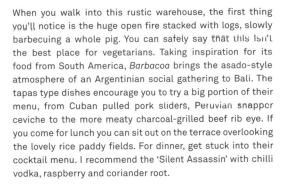

🏠 Jalan Petitenget, 14

☎ +62 81239999825

🢂 barbacoabali.com

✉ info@barbacoabali.com

f Barbacoa

⊙ @barbacoabali

🕑 12pm – 12am

Sardine

13 *Serene Seafood Setting*

Get a feel for the 'old Bali' whist dining next to rice paddy fields in the breezy bamboo structures at *Sardine*. Flocks of ducks run around, dipping in and out of the water while the farmers tend to the rice. Come evening, the fields are softly lit by lights under decorative umbrellas. As the name suggests, *Sardine* focuses mainly on seafood, sourcing their catch from the nearby fishing village of Jimbaran. The menu changes daily due to what's best at the market. You'll be tucking into delightful dishes such as yellowfin tuna carpaccio, pan seared wild snapper and barramundi in banana leaf. This is a lovely place to come for dinner, but you'll need to call in advance to make a reservation, as *Sardine* is a popular spot. Alternatively, pop in for lunch or come for a pre-dinner cocktail when reservations aren't required.

Jalan Petitenget, 21

+62 8113978333

sardinebali.com

sardine@sardinebali.com

Sardine

11.30am – 1am

La Favela

14 *Design Lovers' Drinking Den*

A blink-and-you'll-miss-it entrance hides the enchanting Brazilian inspired bar and restaurant *La Favela*. Walk under leafy vines down an alleyway and into an overgrown cobbled courtyard with tables dotted beneath shady trees. Step beyond the peeling painted doors and you are transported to the living quarters of a family from Rio. Floral laminated cloths cover the dining tables surrounded by mismatched chairs. Kitsch collectibles, faux flowers and framed Virgin Mary pictures decorate the rooms, with 1950's era television sets and pastel coloured cabinets making you feel as if you're hanging out in someone's home. The owners declare that '*Favela*' is a community and welcome people from all walks of life. The food they serve is Mediterranean meets Latin America, while the cocktail menu offers a mix of classics as well as their signature drinks, such as 'Favela Breeze' with peach liqueur and dragon fruit.

🏠 Jalan Laksmana, 177X

☎ +62 361730010

➤ lafavela.com

✉ balilafavela@gmail.com

f La Favela Bali

⭕ lafavelabali_

🕐 12pm – 3am

Motel Mexicola

15 *Kitsch Cocktail Charmer*

Step inside the crazy 1960's world of Latino-loving *Motel Mexicola* and, no, this isn't some seedy Miami-style hotel. Bold, bright and beautiful, this restaurant and bar has endless nooks and corners decorated with hand-painted murals, pots of cactuses and framed photos of tropical loving ladies, like Carmen Miranda. This place is great for a party, so bring along a group of pals and get stuck into their tequila-drenched cocktails and comfort food snacks, such as pork empanadas, chorizo quesadillas and fish tacos. The atmosphere here is friendly and fun, with loud music bouncing off the walls and margaritas flowing from the bar. Show off your moves on the dance floor after a frozen daiquiri or two.

🏠 Jalan Kayu Jati, 9X

📞 +62 361736688

↖ motelmexicolabali.com

📘 Motel Mexicola

📷 @motelmexicola

🕐 12pm – 1am

Potato Head Beach Club

16 *Party in a Pool*

A trip to Bali isn't complete without a good few hours spent propping up the swim-up bar at *Potato Head*. Somewhat of an iconic landmark in Seminyak, *Potato Head* is a huge open air space known best for its long, turquoise infinity pool set beside a stretch of sandy beach. This is a daytime drinking kind of place. The cocktails are masterminded by legendary mixologist Dre Masso, taking inspiration from the venue's tropical location to come up with creations using homemade ingredients like lemongrass gin, vanilla sugar and strawberry foam. If you're planning to be here for a while, you'll want to grab a day bed. Arrive early (before the 11am opening) to ensure you get a spot. Alternatively, you can sit on a submerged bar stool and float around in the pool with a glass of rosé in hand. Classy!

🏠 Jalan Petitenget, 51B

☎ +62 3614737979

🔗 ptthead.com

✉ phbc.reservation@pttfamily.com

📘 Potato Head Beach Club Bali

📷 @pttheadbali

🕐 11am – 2am

Seminyak Flea Market

17 *Bali's Bargains*

I used to dismiss this market, thinking that it was simply a bunch of stalls selling tacky tourist souvenirs and t-shirts with beer brand logos. Okay, so it might have a bit of that as well, but if you look past this you will find a treasure trove of bargains. My first stop is the stand that sells brightly coloured embroidered clutch bags and cushions. You should aim to spend around $10 and $15 respectively on these, but you'll need to haggle here (as well as throughout the market). Stock up on crochet bikinis, shorts, throws and bags that are handmade locally on the island; these should cost you around $10 per piece. Don't miss the lovely stand selling silk kaftans and kimonos – perfect pieces for wafting around the beach bars in.

🏠 Jalan Kayu Aya, near the entrance to *The Oberoi* hotel

⊘ Open every day

Palma Australia

(18) *Affordable Antipodean Style*

If I'm passing through Seminyak and only have time to visit a couple of shops, I'll always pop into *Palma Australia*. It's the place I always take my friends to, to find top quality clothes at modest prices. Located just a couple of doors down from the *Seminyak Flea Market*, this light and airy store stocks their own brand of clothes made in Bali using hand-printed silks and organic cotton. Their vibe could be described as 'fun and fancy beach party attire', with low back jumpsuits made with lace detailing, bohemian floaty dresses and long knitted bodycon dresses. It's a great place to come if you're looking for a unique wedding guest outfit or smart summer gear. For the quality of the clothes the prices are reasonable, and the sale rail is often filled with lovely pieces too.

🏠 Jalan Kayu Aya, 150A

📞 +62 3617809140

🔝 palma-australia.com

📘 Palma Australia

📷 @palmaaustralia

🕐 9.30am – 9pm

Uma & Leopold

19 *Brazil Meets Bali*

Designer Lara Braga moved from her native Rio de Janeiro to live the island life in Bali, where she now works with local craftsmen to produce feminine but edgy summery clothes. Items can take a month to create, using techniques such as Indonesian Karawang embroidery, hand beading and leather weaving. She stocks special pieces to fill up your wardrobe, from silk maxi dresses with lace trimmings, sophisticated shirt dresses to soft structured leather jackets. As well as clothes, *Uma & Leopold* sell stylish shoes, like their platform leather sandals and tanned gladiators. Channel your inner glamazon with their sleek and chic pieces. What you get here is quality craftsmanship at affordable prices.

🏠 Jalan Oberoi, 77X

☎ + 62 361737697

➤ umaandleopold.com

f uma and leopold

📷 @umaandleopold

🕐 9am – 9pm

Lulu Yasmine

20 *Bohemian Handmade Attire*

This Bali-born brand encompasses the nomadic lifestyle — clothes made for girls who hop on adventures around the globe. The travel theme comes from Luiza Chang, a Chinese-Brazilian who grew up in Brazil before living in Europe and then basing herself in Asia. This mix of cultures is reflected in the designs, which are beach-ready resort wear with a nod to European elegance. Inspired by the local craft makers in Bali, the garments are lovingly handmade. Find long silk evening dresses and cream shorts with colourful beaded pockets, alongside French pearly silk lingerie. Some of the prices might be slightly higher than in other stores, but what you're paying for are special one-off pieces for your wardrobe that have been handcrafted on the island.

🏠 Jalan Laksmana, 100X

☎ +62 361736763

↖ luluyasmine.com

f Lulu Yasmine

◉ @luluyasmine

🕒 9am – 9pm

Magali Pascal

21 *Chic Parisian Pieces*

If you're a fan of the elegant stores that line the streets of Paris, then you'll love this French designer's space in Seminyak. One of the higher-end brands in the neighbourhood, *Magali Pascal* (also the name of the designer) stocks stylish and luxurious clothes that are as easy to wear in the city as on the island. Her runway-worthy pieces are designed for special events, such as the couture-style dresses made using sheer lace fabrics and silk chiffon panelling. There are also more everyday outfits like blue and white striped playsuits that would look fitting while walking along the beaches of Biarritz. Pascal has got the Paris meets Bali look down to an art, with vintage inspired light cotton smock dresses and floaty gypsy maxi skirts. Don't miss a look into this bohemian boutique.

Jalan Laksmana, 177X

+62 361736147

magalipascal.com

Magali Pascal

@magalipascal

9am – 10pm

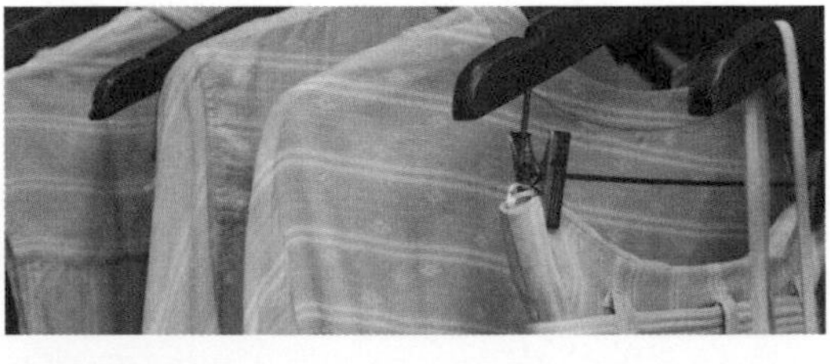

Escalier

22 *Unique Beachwear Brands*

Catering to the international jet-set crowd that flows through the doors of *Potato Head Beach Club*, *Escalier* is a carefully curated store that selects fresh and fun brands from across the globe. With a focus on resort wear, the shop sells swimwear from favourites like Kiini, Fella and Mara Hoffman, playful slogan sunglasses from Wildfox and retro jelly shoes from British brand JuJu. If you've forgotten to pack any sort of beach attire, you can find it here. They've got panama hats, Hawaiian tropics sun cream, towels and beach bags all ready to go for a day by the sea. Perfect if you plan to roll straight off the plane and into *Potato Head* (a routine that many people follow).

🏠 Jalan Petitenget, 51B
(at Potato Head Beach Club)

📞 +62 3613610589

✉ info@escalier-store.com

📘 Escalier

📷 @escalierstore

🕐 11am – 11pm

67

Jalan Raya Kerobokan

23 *Homewares and Furniture Finds*

Dalle Art

If you're after homeware bargains, then get off the main streets of Seminyak with their fancy styled stores and onto the scruffier looking Jalan Raya Kerobokan. One of my favourite shops is *Dalle Art*, where for a couple of Indonesian notes you can pick up a white feather tribal necklace, mermaid-like shell jewellery boxes and mother of pearl trays. Nearby, *Selected Living* sells contemporary wooden furniture and home accessories as well as terracotta pots and weaved baskets. The prices here are very reasonable for the quality and design. There's also a fun shop called *Magic Fish*, which specialises in recycled wood, selling carved doors and colourful curiosities. After visiting these, wander up the road where you'll find more stores selling affordable and one-off items for the home.

 Dalle Art (handicrafts)
Jalan Raya Kerobokan, 80

Selected Living

Magic Fish

Selected Living (home accessories and furniture) Jalan Raya Kerobokan, 115

Magic Fish (recycled wood) Jalan Raya Kerobokan, 120

Bodyworks

(24) *Blissful Urban Oasis*

After pounding the pavements going from shop to shop in Seminyak, you're going to want a bit of pampering. Housed in a light and airy Moroccan riad-style structure, *Bodyworks* is the place to go for a classic day spa experience that Bali is so well known for. Sit outside in the peaceful, plant-filled orange courtyard and be treated to a relaxing foot massage or polished pedicure. They're renowned for their traditional Indonesian healing techniques, from the signature two-hour exfoliation massage, known locally as Mandi Lulur, to hot stone massages using ancient forms of healing. The spa is great value for money, so you can easily spend all afternoon here undergoing treatment after treatment. The vibe of the spa is welcoming to both males and females – so girls, bring along your other half to get their feet scrubbed.

Jalan Kayu Jati, 2

+62 361733317

bodyworksbali.com

Bodyworks Spa Bali

@bodyworksbali

9am – 10pm

Spring

25 *City-Style Spa*

This sleek spa on Jalan Petitenget is the place to go for sophisticated treatments, in what they like to call a 'social spa' environment. *Spring* wouldn't look out of place in cities like New York or London with its minimalistic white interiors and innovative list of therapies. If you've just got off the plane, book yourself in for a 'Jet Away' massage, designed to boost circulation in your swollen feet. If you're going out on the town, they've got a 'Blow wave bar' where you can get a wash, blow-dry and a bohemian braid. Ladies note, this spa is a great place to come and get an emergency pre-beach 'Spring Clean'; they have a full list of leg and bikini waxes and threading. While more fancy than some other spas, *Spring* manages to maintain good-value pricing and feels very professional.

⌂ Jalan Petitenget, 100X

☎ +62 3618499636

↖ springspa.com

f Spring

◎ @spring_spa

◷ 9am – 9pm

Rob Peetoom

26 *Hair Spa with a View*

Dutch hair guru Rob Peetoom hopped over from the Netherlands to open a stylish hair spa in Seminyak. The Asian-inspired buildings have a serene and spiritual energy, whilst feeling über glam. For those precious about their locks, look no further as stylists are trained to exact European standards, so you can get a half-head of highlights or a cut and blow dry with confidence. Offering more than just hair care, for a truly spoiling experience, book yourself in for a pedicure overlooking the tranquil rice paddies. *Rob Peetoom* feels really posh, but luckily the prices are purse friendly so you can have a luxurious experience without the guilt. I'd definitely recommend this place if you want a quiet afternoon of 'me time' in peaceful and plush surroundings.

🏠 Jalan Petitenget, 16

☎ +62 361738363

🏹 robpeetoom.nl

✉ bali@robpeetoom.nl

📘 @robpeetoombali

🕐 Mon – Tues 12pm – 8pm
Wed – Sun 10am – 8pm

Brown Feather

27 *Boutique B&B*

I fondly remember arriving at *Brown Feather* after a jaunt to the Gili Islands (where I stayed at a scruffy backpacker's hostel) and feeling like I'd arrived in heaven. It was also the same price as said hostel, which made me even more impressed. At Rp450k per night, or about $30, *Brown Feather* is amazing value for money. It's a little boutique B&B slightly out of town on Batu Belig, but they give you free use of electric bicycles to whizz into Seminyak in no time. The cast iron beds are beyond comfortable, and I love the vintage Singer sewing machine basins and the all over homely design. If you're in Seminyak for a night or two and want something cheap, cheerful and wonderful then *Brown Feather* is your place.

🏠 Jalan Batu Belig, 100

☎ I 02 0014700100

➤ brownfeather.com

✉ booking@brownfeather.com

📷 @brownfeatherhotel

$ From $30 per night
incl. breakfast

Canggu

Hip and Happening 'Hood

Since the streets of Seminyak have become busier, travellers in the know have decamped to Canggu, the trendy and low-key neighbourhood next door. There's a lovely sense of community here. Being the area of choice for many of the island's expats, the vibe is more akin to a place that people live, rather than a tourist destination. After spending a few days in Canggu, it's easy to feel at home.

Mornings in Canggu start at the crack of dawn, when half the 'hood hop on their bikes down to Batu Bolong or Echo's to tackle the swell. Salty-skinned surfers and golden-limbed honeys then gather over cups of caffeine at one of Canggu's hip coffee hangouts.

While Seminyak is stylish and sophisticated, Canggu is cool and casual. The crowd is young and fun, and there's an atmosphere of creativity and collaboration on every corner. Designers, photographers and artists thrive on the environment of experimentation and opportunity.

Days are spent enjoying lazy lunches by the beach or snacking at healthy organic cafés. Evenings get lively, when cool kids gather to watch guitar-wielding bands.

Book yourself into a breezy open-air villa near the beach with a private pool. Thankfully they're affordable as well as plentiful, so it's easy to find a place to crash even if it's a last minute trip. Seminyak is just a short drive down the shore for more fancy food and bustling bars.

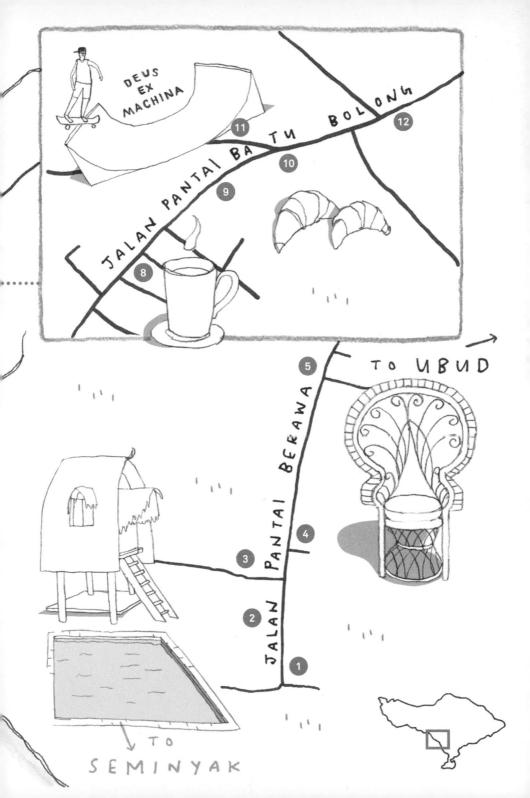

Be Chocolat

1 *Belgium Comes to Bali*

Michel Clement spent his childhood surrounded by the cocoa plantations of the Congo, an experience that shaped his later career as the chocolatier he is today. With his wife, Titus, he decided to move their business from Barcelona to Bali after getting a taste for island life. They've managed to bring the high Belgian standards for chocolate to their little shop on the outskirts of Canggu, sourcing their dark cacao from Sao Tome Island in West Africa and lighter beans locally from Java. Fill a pick 'n' mix box with almond truffles, orange peel covered in dark chocolate, salted chocolate slabs and chocolate sprinkled with chilli. They also have a couple of tables and chairs outside where you can sit and have a chocolate smoothie, hot chocolate or a fondue!

🏠 Jalan Subak Sari, 4

☎ +62 82237414584

f Be Chocolat by Michel Clement

📷 @be_chocolat

🕐 10am – 8pm

Desa Seni

2 *Holistic and Rustic Retreat*

If you want to find the most peaceful place to recharge and revive, pay a visit to the eco village resort of *Desa Seni*. Designed to give you a traditional Indonesian cultural experience, you can stay in an antique wooden bungalow, attend their yoga classes of which there are four a day and be healed at their Svaasthya wellness spa. This 13-roomed retreat is set in a working garden, so you'll see rows of organic vegetables grown on site for use in the restaurant. The Javanese joglo and lumbung accommodation surround a refreshing salt-water pool, which you can laze around in between your yoga and meditation sessions. *Desa Seni* puts on yoga retreats, or as a non-guest you can simply drop in and attend their group yoga classes. Conveniently located, *Desa Seni* is a ten-minute drive away from both central Canggu and Seminyak.

🏠 Jalan Subak Sari, 13

☎ +62 3618446392

🢁 desaseni.com

✉ info@desaseni.com

f Desa Seni

📷 @desaseni

💲 Rooms from $135 incl. breakfast and yoga. Yoga for non-guests: Rp140k.

Milk & Madu

3 *Brunch Stop on Berawa*

🏠 Jalan Pantai Berawa, 52

☎ +62 85102781872

↖ milkandmadu.com

f Milk & Madu

📷 @milkandmadu

🕐 7am – 5pm

This spacious open-air café is a super spot to come for a casual breakfast or brunch on the Berawa strip just outside Canggu. Created by the same people behind *Watercress*, *Milk & Madu* maintains the same level of tasty and healthy food. Being good for you doesn't mean boring though; they've got winners like the burrito breakfast with scrambled eggs and corn salsa avocado, or the super brekky bowl with yoghurt, strawberries, chia seeds and goji berries. The café is in a lovely location, situated beside a garden where wild flowers and baby bananas grow. If you're here for a pit stop, *Milk & Madu* have a great choice of drinks, from green kale juices to delicious coconut water with lychee.

Bungalow Living

4 *Lovely Lifestyle Store*

Bungalow Living is a heavenly homeware store that cleverly doubles up as a charming café. The space is styled like you're in the home of someone really fabulous, and of course the best bit is you can buy all the lovely things that you see on the shelves. Stock up on pom pom fringed embroidered cushions, Indian cotton bed linen, handmade banana leaf storage baskets and colourful quilts. There are cosy corners in the café where you can sit down for a coffee or dragon fruit super smoothie while deciding on how much you can take home in your suitcase. Opposite the café is the Bungalow gallery, where you can find bigger pieces such as white peacock chairs, decorative birdcages and wall art. *Bungalow Living* is a great shop to find gifts for friends or to kit out your home.

🏠 Jalan Pantai Berawa, 35A

☎ +62 3618446567

🔖 bungalowlivingbali.com

📘 Bungalow Living Bali

📷 @bungalowlivingcafe

🕐 8.30am – 6pm

Campur Asia

5 *Delicious Japanese Deli*

With its blink-and-you'll-miss-it location just up the road from *Bungalow Living* on Berawa, *Campur Asia* is a small and casual deli frequented by foodies in the know. This low-key dining spot is rooted in Japanese and Asian home cooking. The focus is on fresh and flavoursome food, with dishes like Thai green curry noodle soup, ahi poke bowl with raw tuna, and Vietnamese spring rolls on the menu. For an extra boost, you can slurp wheatgrass shots knocked back with homemade lemon ice tea or a mango berry frappé. The design is cosy and slightly kitsch, with mismatched outdoor seating and a newer, cooler indoor area. They also have a display of colourful vintage Asian crockery on sale for you to take home with you.

🏠 Jalan Pantai Berawa, 17

☎ +62 3618868787

↖ campurasia.com

⊘ Mon – Sat 11am – 7pm

Old Man's

6 *Happening Beach Hangout*

After a couple of days spent in Canggu, you'll feel yourself naturally gravitating back to *Old Man's* time and time again. This place is sort of everything for everyone. Early bird surfers can roll in here straight out of the water, rinse under the outdoor showers and then fill up on bacon and egg rolls or banana porridge. If you're with a group of friends, come here for a lazy lunch and graze on good old burgers and chips washed down with a couple of glasses of wine. The food is simple pub grub, but the prices are good and it's an easy-going, relaxed environment. Come evening, perch under a palm tree on one of their wooden benches for a sunset cocktail or two. Do look out for the market, held on the last Saturday of the month. You'll find one-off vintage clothes and statement jewellery as well as freshly-baked cakes.

🏠 Jalan Pantai Batu Bolong
(by the beach)

☎ +62 3618469158

📘 Old Man's

📷 @oldmansbali

🕐 7am – 12am

Batu Bolong Beach

7 *Black Sand Beach*

 Jalan Pantai Batu Bolong

A world away from the white coloured beaches of The Bukit, Canggu has the more typical Balinese volcanic black sand lining its shores. Batu Bolong Beach is best known amongst the surfers that paddle in from early morning 'til dusk. It's also a spot for the local surf camps that reside in Canggu — there are plenty around if you want to step up your surf game over a week or so. There are stacks of boards for hire by the beach and surf instructors on hand for lessons too. With the current being so strong it isn't advised for swimmers, so it's perhaps best to paddle, lounge around on the beach or go for a barefoot stroll. Pop into *Old Man's* just behind the beach for a bite to eat and shade from the midday sun.

Crate Café

8 *Life's Crate at this Cool Café*

Crate Café has to be the coolest kid on the block, with its SoundCloud beats blaring out, and hip young things with nose piercings and five panel caps hopping off their motorbikes to gather at this neighbourhood meeting spot. Like any café in Bali worth its salt, *Crate* is serious about their coffee and serves up an in-house blend. The breakfasts are just as strong. With names like 'Why So Cereal' (frozen banana and goodies), 'Hipstar' acai bowls and 'Goldilocks' porridge, this place is all about being young and fun. This busy and buzzing brunch venue attracts Canggu's creative crowd, who talk collaborations over their flat whites and iced shakerato coffees. With their motto 'Life's Crate', I know where I'll be spending my mornings in Bali.

🏠 Jalan Pantai Batu Bolong, 64

☎ +62 81238943040

📘 Crate Café

📷 @cratecafe

🕑 7am – 3pm

Betelnut Café

9 *Healthy, Hearty, Happy Food*

If there was any doubt that healthy organic food could not be filling and tasty, *Betelnut Café* can show you how it's done. Walk up the wooden steps and into the tree house-like set up, with lovely views looking over the green rice paddy fields of Canggu. This little café is one popular hangout, with tables filled with detoxing yoga bunnies, surfers needing an energy fix and cool young families. This is one of my favourite places for lunch. I'll always go for the 'Big Betelnut' salad and dragon fruit smoothie, and I can never resist the raw raspberry chocolate cheesecake! An all-day joint open for breakfast, lunch and dinner, they also have a hearty Mexican menu of mahi mahi fish tacos and chicken burritos for those that want a bigger fill.

🏠 Jalan Pantai Batu Bolong, 60

☎ +62 82146807233

📘 Betelnut Cafe

📷 @betelnutcafe

🕐 7am – 10pm

Monsieur Spoon

10 *Flavoursome French Bakery*

Masterminded by a Parisian pastry chef, *Monsieur Spoon* is a small French bakery filling that croissant-shaped hole in the Canggu breakfast scene. Pop in for a classic combo of coffee, flaky croissants and jam, fill up on avocado and eggs or tuck into a traditional Croque-Madame. The founders are passionate about using top quality ingredients in their food, whether it's an almond chocolatine or a pistachio macaroon. Be careful though, a regular routine of starting your day at *Monsieur Spoon* can soon become an addiction. I have a friend who banned himself from here to avoid an expanding waistline. I probably shouldn't tell you that the café also delivers (number listed). It's a dangerous place for anyone working on his or her beach body.

🏠 Jalan Pantai Batu Bolong, 55

☎ +62 87862808859

🔖 monsieurspoon.com

📘 Monsieur Spoon

📷 @monsieurspoon

🕐 6am – 9pm

Deus Ex Machina

11 *Bikes, Boards, Brunch and Bands*

Deus (pronounced 'day us') is a creative den for those that like to get high on caffeine and gasoline. The main warehouse is filled with beefy motorbikes, custom shaped boards and racks of graphic printed t-shirts (for those of us not cool enough for the main items on sale). Come here to browse the bikes, and stay for brunch and coffee in the so-called 'Temple of Enthusiasm'. If you like to get inked, make sure you're around for their 'Tacos 'n' Tatt Tuesdays', when you can get tequilas and complimentary tattoos on tap. Sunday nights are where it's at, when the whole of Canggu descends on *Deus* to watch raucous live bands and drink beer and mojitos.

🏠 Jalan Pantai Batu Mejan, 8

☎ +62 811388315

🔗 deuscustoms.com

📘 Deus Bali

📷 @deustemple

🕐 8am – 10pm

Lacalita

12 *Cocktails and Ceviche*

A laid back and funky Mexican restaurant on Batu Bolong, *Lacalita* is a great dinner option for fresh and filling food paired with killer cocktails. The design of the restaurant is bold and beautiful, with flower pom poms hanging off the ceiling, a range of rainbow coloured chairs and walls decorated with Central American inspired pictures. Try tasty portions of ceviche and avocado, grilled corn, guacamole with homemade nachos, and tacos carnitas – slow braised pork shoulder with pineapple salsa. Don't leave without ordering the sugarcoated churros with melted hot chocolate sauce for dessert. It's a great place to come with a group of friends; get stuck into their drinks menu containing all the classics – frozen strawberry daiquiris, Bloody Marys and margaritas.

🏠 Jalan Pantai Batu Bolong, 68

☎ +62 82247312217

f Lacalita

📷 @lacalitabali

🕐 Mon – Fri 10am – 11pm. Sat – Sun 8am – 11pm.

Echo Beach

13 *Quiet Surfers' Spot*

Known locally as Pantai Batu Mejan, Echo Beach is similar to its neighbouring beach, Batu Bolong, with its black volcanic sand and surf-worthy waves. A scattering of simple warungs and a couple of restaurants line the shore, serving up local Indonesian food and seafood BBQs come evening. Big, comfy beanbags, sun loungers and umbrellas are dotted on the sand so you can chill and watch the surfers at play. Although the beach isn't your idyllic, tropical postcard perfection, it's quiet and uncrowded, and there's something quite unique about the black sand under your feet. A popular place for surfers, the waves can be quite rough for swimmers, although it's nice for a shallow paddle. 'Echo's', as it's called, is a lovely place to come for a couple of beers come sunset.

🏠 Jalan Pantai Batu Mejan

Villa Phoenix

14 *Beautiful Boho Surf Pad*

This bohemian hideaway is positioned a stone's throw away from Echo Beach – close enough to hear the waves crashing while you lounge by the pool, and if you hop up to the second floor balcony you're in a good position to do a surf check. A two-bedroom villa that can be rented by the room, what strikes you is the amount of design and detail that has gone into making this place a home. The villa is filled with art found locally in Bali as well as artefacts picked up from around the world. The whole space is designed for outdoor living, from the wall-less kitchen and living room, to the lush green plants dotted in every corner. Staff is on hand to cook your morning banana pancakes, and dog lovers will be delighted by the live-in host, 'Kiss Kiss', their puppy.

🏠 Echo Beach

🢅 airbnb.com/rooms/899419

$ From $94 per night per room incl. breakfast

Spiritual and Serene Jungle Hideaway

Ubud is best known as the spiritual centre of Bali. Located in the heart of the island, it has long attracted the arty types drawn to its rich cultural heritage. The area surrounding Ubud is gorgeously green. Think thick foliage weaving down river valleys and chirpy birds singing in the treetops in a jungle-like setting.

The people here are artists, spiritual healers, yoga teachers and chefs who live in Ubud for the lifestyle, which is all about simplicity and being close to nature.

Home to a burgeoning festival scene in literature, music, the arts and food, Ubud has become a meeting point in Asia for like-minded souls who have a shared interest in celebrating culture.

The culinary scene is constantly evolving, with top Indonesian and international chefs setting up their kitchens here with a focus on working with the local community to source farm-fresh ingredients.

Traditional Balinese craftsmen, with skills passed down through generations, hold steady. Pockets of expert wood carvers, silversmiths and mask makers can be found in the villages around Ubud. Their passion and love for their art is untainted, and for me it is one of the most special aspects of the area.

Similar to Seminyak, Ubud's popularity has meant that this once small village has developed into a proper town. I therefore suggest you stay outside central Ubud in an adjacent village — I love staying in Penestanan or in a jungle hideaway in Tegalalang.

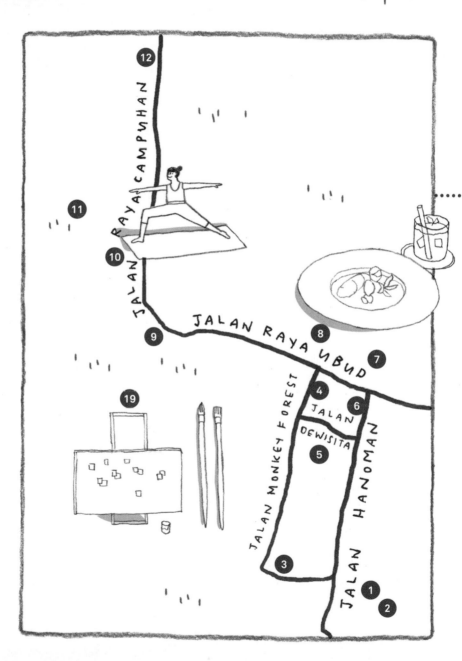

UBUD

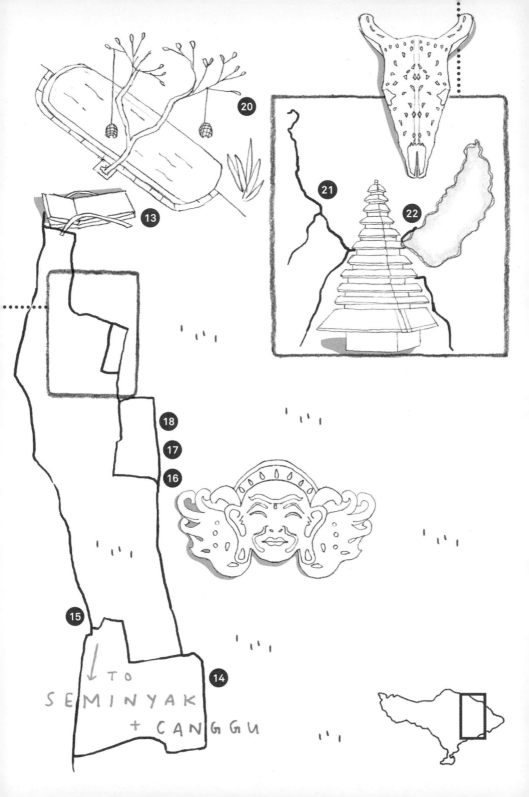

20

13

21

22

18

17

16

15

14

→ TO
SEMINYAK
+ CANGGU

Yoga Barn

① *Holistic Healing Hangout*

🏠 Jalan Pengosekan

☎ +62 361971236

↖ theyogabarn.com

✉ info@theyogabarn.com

f The Yoga Barn - Bali

⊙ @theyogabarn

⊘ 7am – 9pm

More than simply a space to come and practice your tree pose, *Yoga Barn* is an action-packed community centre for the spiritually inclined. It's the sort of place where you'll drop in for a session of Vinyasa Flow and then stumble into Tibetan bowl meditation, before sipping on a green juice at the *Garden Kafe*. This place is so relaxed that the toughest decision you will have to make is whether to fill your afternoon with community astrology or Yin Yoga Healing. While *Yoga Barn* is situated centrally in Ubud town, it maintains that quiet, countryside feel due to its location surrounded by lush green rice fields and willowy palm trees. It's the perfect place to come on your own for a bit of time out, and you can also stay on site in their guesthouse accommodation. Anyone can drop in to one of *Yoga Barn's* hourly classes, priced at Rp120k a go.

Kush

2 *Amazing Ayurvedic Therapies*

THE place for the most marvelous Ayurvedic massages, *Kush* is the spa outpost of the spiritual sanctuary *Yoga Barn*. *Kush* or 'Koosh', meaning happiness in Sanskrit, was recommended to me by an Ayurveda-loving friend, and I'm pretty pleased that she did. I went for a whole body 'Relaxing Abhyanga Massage', and it could have easily been one of the most calming and tranquil 60 minutes I've ever had. They use warm and wonderfully smelling oils, which aim to increase circulation, promote lymphatic draining and to preserve a youthful, vital and supple body – great! The massage huts are beside the river, so you can hear the soft, soothing sound of the water rushing below you. With massages priced from Rp270k a session, it's tempting to come here every day for a dose of bliss – I'd strongly advise it.

 Jalan Pengosekan
(at Yoga Barn)

 +62 361971236

 theyogabarn.com/kush

 kush@theyogabarn.com

 9am – 7pm

Hubud

③ *Work-Life Balance*

While I'm not encouraging you to work while on holiday, if you work remotely or for yourself, there's no better place to do this than Bali. *Hubud* is part of the growing global co-working space movement, and it draws creative entrepreneurs from all over the world. It really is one of the most incredible places you could call an office, with its breezy bamboo structure and everyday scenes like children flying their kites in the field in front of you. The on site café, *Living Food Lab*, is slightly more exciting than your average office canteen, offering raw treats, juices and fruit smoothies. There is a strong community aspect to *Hubud*, where members collaborate and help each other, and there's always inspiring events and courses held throughout each month.

🏠 Jalan Monkey Forest, 88X

☎ +62 361978073

↖ hubud.org

✉ team@hubud.org

f Hubud: Ubud coworking community space

⊙ @hubudbali

$ From $60 per month

Locavore

4 *Locally-Sourced Fare*

🏠 Jalan Dewi Sita, 1

☎ +62 361977733

🖱 restaurantlocavore.com

✉ reservations@
resaurantlocavore.com

📘 Restaurant Locavore

🕐 12pm – 3pm, 6pm – 11pm

If there is one restaurant you need to visit in Bali, it's *Locavore*. The chefs at the helm, Ray (Indonesian) and Eelke (Dutch), have created a clever concept where innovative European dishes are produced using local ingredients. During the seven-course tasting menu you might have cold crab salad with fennel mayonnaise, pan-fried scallops and Jerusalem artichoke sauce, or organically-fed pork with mulberry jus. The dessert is divine; I loved the warm milk chocolate mousse and passion fruit sorbet with raw cacao brittle. They also have a Herbivore tasting menu for vegetarians. Note: due to *Locavore's* popularity you will need to book at least a few weeks in advance, which can be done on their website. Do check out their casual breakfast/lunch spot, *Locavore To Go*, on the same road.

Pica

(5) *South American Kitchen*

Run by the most delightful duo, Cristian and Monica, *Pica* serves up South American dishes inspired by the chef's home country of Chile. Housed in a small and unassuming open-air structure on the main Dewi Sita strip, the experience at *Pica* is casual and personal. Choose from a carefully curated menu of Ceviche Nikkeo (lime marinated mahi-mahi, red onion and coriander), Causa del Mar (octopus, prawns and mahi escabeche on Peruvian cold potato cake) or Cerdo con Manzana (confit pork belly and roasted sweet potatoes). The wine list here is super, stocking new world wines from South America as well as Australia and New Zealand. Save space for their dessert; I loved the Leche Asada (Chilean crème caramel).

🏠 Jalan Dewi Sita

☎ +62 361971660

➤ picakitchen.co

✉ welcome@picakitchen.co

❟ PICA South American Kitchen

⊘ Tues – Sun 6pm – 11pm
Open for lunch during
high season.

Kevala Ceramics

6 *Handcrafted Homewares*

During a meal at *Locavore* I couldn't help but marvel at the beautiful plates, bowls and cups they were using to serve their food on. To my delight I found that they source their tableware locally from *Kevala Ceramics*, and the shop was just across the road! The word Kevala in Sanskrit means perfect, whole and complete, and the ceramics are entirely handmade by local artisans in Bali. The products they sell are stunning and will make any meal you create at home look really fancy. I bought a whole cupboard's worth of plates, vases and bowls to take with me on the plane home. It is amazing value for the quality you get and beats the mass produced factory stuff in the shops. As well as the Ubud branch, you can also stock up at their shop in Seminyak.

🏠 Jalan Dewi Sita

☎ +62 3614792532

🔝 kevalaceramics.com

📘 Kevala Ceramics

📷 @kevalaceramics

🕘 9.30am – 7.30pm

Hujan Locale

7 *Modern Indonesian Cuisine*

From the people behind Seminyak's *Mama San*, *Hujan Locale* is a contemporary restaurant celebrating innovative Indonesian cuisine. Its roots lie in its relationship with local farmers and the surrounding community. With most of the higher-end restaurants in Bali offering international cuisine, it's refreshing to visit a venue that stays true to its home country. Start off with the super tasty cocktails – I like 'Hujan Day' with Gin rosso, lemon, vanilla, Tabasco and cucumber. The Asian-inspired dishes are designed for sharing, so order large and get a taste of the Indonesian islands with dishes like Sulawesi salt baked baby barramundi, Sumatran barbequed pork ribs and East Java tahu tek with petis bean sprouts. A great place to come for dinner, and it's open for lunch too.

🏠 Jalan Sri Wedari, 5

☎ +62 3618493092

🏹 hujanlocale.com

✉ reservations@hujanlocale.com

📘 Hujan Locale

📷 @hujan_locale

🕐 12pm – 11pm

Ibu Oka

8 *Roast Pig Feast*

Jalan Tagal Sari, 2
(behind Ubud Palace)

11am – 3pm

This local eating spot has built up quite the fan base –
mildly helped by the fact that the famous American chef
Anthony Bourdain once featured *Ibu Oka* in an episode of
'No Reservations' where he declared 'this is the best pig I've
ever had!' *Ibu Oka* serves up the traditional Indonesian dish
of roasted babi guling, or suckling pig, stuffed with herbs
and spices and cooked over an open flame. I personally
feel that it does live up to the hype, and I never leave Ubud
without a visit to this pork-filled canteen. It has recently
been renovated to fit more hungry customers so it's slightly
lost its rustic feel, although do ask if you can have a look out
the back, where you'll see whole pigs turning on spits next to
piles of logs ready to feed the fire. Come here for lunch; it's
good value and extremely tasty.

Alchemy

9 *Heavenly Healthy Café*

If there's anywhere that can convince you to change your meat-eating ways and become a fully-fledged vegan, it's *Alchemy*. Healthy without being too hippie, *Alchemy* offers a delicious and inventive menu where your California maki sushi and nacho chips taste like the real deal. Their main event is the raw salad bar, with a serious line up including zucchini noodles, cucumber salsa and almond croutons – enough to make the most devout vegan foodie shriek with glee. Their sweets and desserts particularly impressed me, so I couldn't help but have three! Cloud 9 Cake does what is says on the tin – a light vanilla cheesecake with raspberry topping, and I'm still not sure how it's dairy free. They have a mighty long drinks menu with every fruit- and veg-filled juice under the sun, which they serve with a clever eco papaya stem straw.

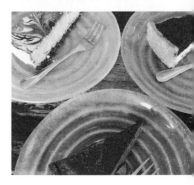

🏠 Jalan Penestanan Kelod, 75

☎ +62 361971981

🔖 alchemybali.com

📘 Alchemy

📷 @alchemybali

🕐 7am – 9pm

Intuitive Flow

10 *Scenic Yoga Studio*

With its walls of windows enabling visitors to look over the valleys of Ubud and out to the distant volcanoes, this might just be one of the most scenic studios you'll have the chance to practice yoga in. *Intuitive Flow* is located in the artists' village of Penestanan and is quite off the beaten track so can be hard to find, but it's worth the search and it also generally means that the classes are uncrowded. The atmosphere here is intimate and welcoming. It is a lovely place to come for a morning yoga session, when the sunrise light floods through the glass. Afterwards, pop into the nearby *Yellow Flower Café* for fresh juices and organic food. Drop-in yoga classes are Rp120k.

🏠 Jalan Raya Tjampuhan, Penestanan

☎ +62 361977824

↖ intuitiveflow.com

✉ contact@intuitiveflow.com

f Intuitive Flow Yoga Studio

◷ 7am – 7pm

Passiflora

11 *Dreamy Javanese Joglo*

If you want a totally unique lodging experience in the Ubud area, look no further than the wonderful *Passiflora*. Located in the quiet rice paddy fields in the artists' village of Penestanan, *Passiflora* is a 100-year-old antique wooden joglo. Masterminded by Alejandra, a Bali based Argentine-American architect, who personally visits Java to seek out these beautiful buildings and brings them back piece by piece to be reassembled. Everything about this home – from the carved blue washed wooden walls, the peaceful position five minutes walk from any road, the lush greenery surrounding it, to the salt water pool – is a total dream. The gorgeous bathroom is outdoors and surrounded by plants, so it's like having a bath in a little jungle. Staff is on hand to make you plates of fruit and toast for breakfast, and they can even organise a spoiling in-joglo massage.

🏠 Penestanan, Ubud

🖱 airbnb.com/rooms/58045

$ $170 per night incl. breakfast

Room 4 Dessert

12 *Candy-Coated Creations*

🏠 Jalan Raya Sanggingan

☎ +62 81236662806

🢑 room4dessert.asia

✉ room4dessertubud@gmail.com

📘 Room4Dessert Ubud

📷 @room4dessert_wg

🕑 Mon – Sat 6pm – 1am

Calling all sweet-toothed travellers, don't miss out on an evening of culinary entertainment at the marvelous sugar-infused restaurant *Room 4 Dessert*. Will Goldfarb is the charismatic chef behind this divine joint. Originally from New York, his restaurant of the same name was the IT place in town, with celebrities like director Wes Anderson his regulars. Lured by the Ubud lifestyle, he set up camp in this unique spot where he treats customers to a tasting menu of nine carefully crafted sweet snacks paired with a selection of fine wines. Dessert dishes include Wu-Tang Clan inspired 'Ghostface Keller' (with Reblochon, 'Bintang' focaccia, cocoa nibs and roasted papaya) and 'Taro Card' (with jackfruit, caramelized coconut milk, passion fruit and pumpkin seeds). If you're looking for something savoury, pop into their secret back garden, where you'll find *L'Hort*: a Catalan-inspired snack bar serving Jamon Iberico and Spanish Tortilla.

Alam Ubud

13 *Peaceful Jungle Hideaway*

This is one of those gems that friends have begged me not to share, but after all my visits to Bali this is still one of my favourite places to stay. You see, there are plenty of fancy and expensive hotels around, but for me *Alam Ubud* has everything you could want. Located 9km north of Ubud in the Tegalalang area, it's unbelievably peaceful and beyond beautiful and, with rooms or 'villas' from $120 a night, it's a total steal. There are only 20 villas at the hotel, with many of them having their own pools so it's all very private, and you'll often have the main pool to yourself. Yoga classes are held in the valley by the flowing river, and they do fab cooking lessons where you can learn to make local dishes like chicken satay, sambal and nasi goreng.

🏠 Desa Kendran, Tegalalang

☎ +62 8970901009

⤷ alamubudvilla.com

✉ info@alamubudvilla.com

$ From $120 incl. breakfast

Celuk Silver Village

 Handcrafted Silver Jewellery

The village of Celuk, 11km south of Ubud, is the centre for silversmiths in Bali. The skills of the local artists have been passed down through generations; most inhabitants of Celuk are part of jeweller families and silversmiths themselves. I suggest you visit the shop *Rama Sita*, which is a wonderful gallery with a workshop on site that promotes the wares of local artists. The items on sale here are some of the highest quality works of craftsmanship you will see. My favourite item was a hand carved wooden bowl with an intricately designed silver snake wrapped around it – totally unique! If you take a look out the back you can see the talented silversmiths in action, crafting the most beautiful and detailed pieces of art.

Rama Sita

 Rama Sita, Jalan Raya Celuk

 +62 361298054

Guide
I suggest using a driver to visit the artists' villages, as they can be tricky to find. I recommend Putu Arnawa, who is a very knowledgeable Bali guide.

 balifriend.com

 putuarnawa@aol.com

Batubulan Stone Carving Village

15 *Symbolic Stone Sculptures*

🏠 Jalan Raya Singapadu, Batubulan

During your travels around Bali you will be sure to notice the many stone sculptures that decorate temples and palaces and adorn the gateways to homes. The main stone-carving village is Batubulan, some 14km south of Ubud and not far from Celuk, the silver village. If you stop by at one of the roadside stands you can see the master carvers at work. Using sandstone, limestone from Java and 'paras' (the grey volcanic sand), the craftsmen tirelessly work to produce these fine sculptures. These are not for the tourist market but instead are sold locally to Balinese people for temples and homes. Even though they are beautiful works of art, they are simply too heavy and expensive to ship internationally. Note that there are varying degrees of quality; in some cases a mold is used, producing a cheaper product that makes the stone look too smooth. In contrast, the high quality stonework will have been carefully carved by hand and have a more artistic finish.

Mas Wood Carving

16 *Unique Wooden Shapes*

As the central Ubud stores increasingly hawk mass-produced souvenirs, you'll need to travel slightly outside of town to the village of Mas to find the real deal. A short 5km south from Ubud town, Mas is known best for its wood carving crafts. The pioneer of the local scene was a man named Ida Bagus Tilem. You can visit a lovely museum run by his sons called the *Njana Tilem Gallery*, which depicts stunning works representing everyday life in Bali, be it farmers or fishermen, frozen in wood. I also recommend visiting I W Mudana's studio, where you can see Mudana's own unique style of carving using irregular shaped wood with twists and holes. He has rooms full of stunning works, known for their spiraling heights and individuality.

Njana Tilem Gallery

🏠 Jalan Raya Mas

☎ +62 361975099

✉ njanatilemgallery@yahoo.co.id

I W Mudana

🏠 Br. Batanancak, Mas

☎ +62 361974549

✉ mudana.master@gmail.com

Mas Mask Making

17 *Magical Masks*

If you are looking for a truly special token to take home with you to remember your time in Bali, I suggest you visit I Wayan Muka's mask-making studio in Mas to pick up one of his unique creations. Like most craftsmen on the island, his skills have been passed down through generations. You can see the whole process, from the blocks of wood he uses to carve the faces, to the beautiful finished products displayed on the walls. The amount of time and skill that goes into making a mask is unbelievable; one piece can use up to 350 coats of paint to make it a finished product. The masks are traditionally used in ceremonial dancing, with some items dedicated just for this purpose and not for public sale.

I Wayan Muka

 Br Batancak, Mas

 +62 361974530

 spiritofmask@yahoo.com

Mas Antique Furniture

(18) *Joyful Javanese Furniture*

For those of you that go weak at the knees at the sight of brightly-coloured Indonesian doors and think it's perfectly practical to want to sleep in an antique Balinese day bed, I've found just the place for you. Best known for its tradition of woodcarving, Mas is also home to a collection of lovely antique and wooden furniture shops. My favourite store of them all is *Tan Celagi*, which stocks antique joglo furniture sourced from Java. Think 20ft-wide carved wooden walls, turquoise coloured screens and intricately painted tall wooden doors. They work with international shipping companies to make that impulse buy that bit easier. There are rows of shops along this road selling more wooden furniture like *Jati Mas*, which sells doors galore.

Tan Celagi

🏠 Jalan Raya Mas

☎ +62 81392513920

✉ tancelagi@yahoo.com

Penestanan Young Artists

19 *Artists' Neighbourhood*

Penestanan is a little village next to the main Ubud town. It is known as the 'Young Artist's Village' due to the community of artists that formed here during the 1900s. European artists came to Bali and started working alongside local painters where a new style of work was formed. You can still see this genre of painting when visiting local artists, such as the much admired I Ketut Soki. It's a special experience visiting the home and studio of this artist. He has beautiful finished works depicting daily island life: traditional ceremonies, dancing and farming – all illustrated using bold, bright colours. To learn more about this artists' movement, visit the nearby *Neka Art Museum*, which shows a great collection of varying local works with accompanying information.

I Ketut Soki

🏠 Penestanan Kelod

☎ +62 361974370

Neka Art Museum

🏠 Raya Campuhan St.

☎ +62 361975074

🔗 museumneka.com

Tampak Siring Bone Carving village

20 *The Bone Collector*

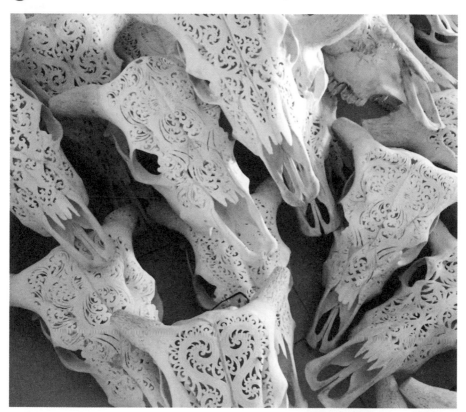

You may see examples of bull and buffalo skull carvings appearing in shops on your travels around Bali, but I suggest making a trip up to the specialist 'Bone Carving' village of Tampak Siring to see the masters at work and to support them at the source. The quiet village streets are dotted with storefronts where you can meet the bone carvers themselves. Ask kindly and they may let you into their workshop behind their store. Visiting the artisans themselves means that you have a greater choice of what's on offer, and most do custom orders so you can come with your own design to have hand carved into the skulls. Shops offer varying prices, but as a benchmark look to pay Rp500k for a piece. I'd recommend the shop *Ida Bagus Tantra* for good quality and price. Nearby is the sacred 'Tirta Empul Temple' famous for its holy water, so you can also stop off to see this while you're here.

Ida Bagus Tantra

 Br. Penaka, Tampak Siring

Mount Batur

21 *Volcano Views*

Mount Batur is a 1,700m high active volcano in the north east of Bali. Located 35km north of Ubud, the scenic journey there takes around an hour to drive, passing orchards of mandarin orange trees and piles of fruit for sale on the sides of the road. Head towards the highland village of Kintamani, which sits on the rim of the Batur caldera, where you can see the most stunning views of Mount Batur and Lake Batur. There are numerous cafés with viewing decks that you can stop at to have a drink and enjoy the scenery. A popular activity is the trek to the summit of Mount Batur at sunrise: a two-hour climb that starts at around 2am and can be organised with a guide. I definitely recommend a trip here any time of the day to see one of Bali's most beautiful spots.

Getting here
From Ubud, head 35km north towards the village of Kintamani.

Lake Batur Temple

22 *Temple on the Lake*

After you've admired the views of Mount Batur from the heights of Kintamani, you should carry on your journey down to the deep crater lake and visit the quiet temple called Pura Segara Lake Batur. When I came here in the afternoon there wasn't anyone around – just a fisherman rowing his boat on the lake next to the temple. It's a lovely experience: very peaceful and serene. The almost floating temple can be viewed from the riverbank or you can cross the rickety bridge to see it up close. This temple isn't on the main tourist trail, and there isn't a ticketing office or the general bustle of the busier temples. Do take a trip here before it becomes a visitor hotspot; there aren't many of these places left!

Getting here
From Ubud, head 35km north towards the village of Kintamani. From here carry on driving along Jalan Raya Penelokan until you see the left turning down to the lake. Note that this is a bumpy road.

Nusa Lembongan

Beautiful Beaches and Wild Waves

A cluster of islands situated off the south east coast of Bali, Nusa Lembongan and its sisters Nusa Ceningan and Nusa Penida are a quieter and more rustic alternative to mainland Bali. Nusa Lembongan, which can be reached by a 30-minute boat ride from the town of Sanur, is the more developed of the three, with more choice of accommodation and restaurants.

Roads are bumpy, and there aren't any cars but a few transport trucks used by resorts. Travellers meander around the islands of Lembongan and Ceningan on mopeds: the best way to get around.

The main activities on these islands are snorkeling and surfing. Days are laid back, simple and always with a dose of adventure. Beach hopping is a must. It is made all the more idyllic as you slowly pass by seaweed strewn on the roadside drying under the sun and wooden fishing boats floating in turquoise waters.

The beaches on the island are beautiful, although looks can be deceiving — be careful of the currents and avoid stepping into some waters altogether. What you'll see is your typical tropical island scenes. Willowy palm trees and rugged rocks frame cream-coloured sands.

Nusa Lembongan and its sister islands are rougher around the edges compared to their more popular counterpart. Don't expect fine dining; instead park up on the waterfront at a local Indonesian warung with a smoky grill of fresh snapper with sambal sauce, rice and chicken satay. Nusa Lembongan is best for a short trip; I'd say two or three days would do.

8

Sandy Bay Beach Club

1 *Scenic Beach Restaurant*

This all-day dining hangout has the most scenic setting on Sunset Beach, which can be found on the south west of Nusa Lembongan Island. *Sandy Bay Beach Club* is a stylishly rustic and laid-back restaurant and bar, serving up crowd-pleasing grub like burgers and BBQ grilled seafood. It's a lovely place to come for lunch, where you can wander on the white sand before settling in for a long and lazy eating session. They have a good selection of wines and fruit cocktails on their menu too. As the name of the beach suggests, it's a gorgeous spot for sunset, where the falling sun glistens on the wild waves. *Sandy Bay* also has a boutique filled with bikinis and summer dresses, and there's a spa for post-lunch pampering.

🏠 Sunset Beach, Nusa Lembongan

☎ +62 82897005656

↖ sandybaylembongan.com

✉ tbc@sandybaylembongan.com

f Sandy Bay Beach Club

⊘ 8am – 10pm

Villa Voyage

2 *Beachfront Party Pad*

It can be hard to find nice accommodation on Nusa Lembongan, so if you want comfort and space I'd always suggest a villa. When you gather a group of friends together even the most luxurious of pads can be affordable. *Villa Voyage* must be one of the best, and with five bedrooms it works out at a reasonable $100 per head if you have a full house, and this includes staff and a chef. The villa is located right on the beautiful Sunset Beach, neighbouring *Sandy Bay Beach Club*. The design is barefoot luxury; all bedrooms have en-suite bathrooms and a contemporary safari chic vibe. There are some other lovely villas surrounding this beach – have a look at the three-bedroom *Island House* next door if you want something slightly smaller.

Villa Voyage

🔖 villavoyagebali.com

💲 From $995 per night

Island House

🔖 nusalembonganvillas.com

💲 From $300 per night

Dream Beach

3 *White Sand Wonderland*

Just around the corner from Sunset Beach is another one of Nusa Lembongan's picture-postcard scenes – Dream Beach. Quiet and uncrowded, this beauty spot attracts a handful of travellers in the know. The soft sand is an idyllic cream colour and the water a dazzling aqua hue. I was lured in for a dip by the tempting ocean colours, but be warned that the current is strong so swimming isn't advised (I quickly got out!). There's a casual café by the beach for lunch. Go upstairs to the top deck where they have comfy day beds perfect for an afternoon spent getting stuck into your holiday read, with stunning aerial views over Dream Beach. If you want to stay on the beach, there is a sprinkling of simple Balinese lumbung huts metres from the sand for a no-frills sleeping experience.

 Dream Beach,
Nusa Lembongan

Mushroom Bay

4 *Sunset Spot*

Mushroom Bay on the west of Nusa Lembongan has calmer waters compared to its neighbouring beaches. The plus side of this is that it's swimmer friendly although you'll need to time your visit to the beach right. During the day boats full of visitors descend to do sporting activities on its placid waters, so come here past 3pm when it's lovely and quiet again. The vibe is peaceful and relaxed, with a mix of families and couples propped up on beanbags on the sand, ready to admire the stunning sunset that falls on the water on the bay. There's a bamboo structured restaurant *Hai Bar & Grill* where you can get a glass of wine, a cocktail and simple dishes like pizza and calamari. Come to Mushroom Bay for a late afternoon laze around.

🏠 Mushroom Bay, Nusa Lembongan

Seaweed Farmers

5 *Local Life*

Hop on a bike and head to the most southern point of Nusa Lembongan where you will find a bright yellow suspension bridge that connects to Nusa Ceningan (Nusa Lembongan's smaller and quieter neighbour). When you start your journey around this island, one of the first things you will notice is the abundance of green seaweed that has been harvested and is lying out on sheets of tarpaulin on the roadside, drying under the blazing sun. While Bali has its rice, Ceningan has its seaweed, and this has traditionally been the island's main industry. It's nice to stop and see what people are up to, and it's interesting to see a different side to what the locals do which isn't about tourism. I found those I approached to be warm, smiley and friendly. In fact, a couple of ladies I went up to couldn't stop laughing (probably at me).

Getting here
From Nusa Lembongan, head south and look for the yellow bridge that links to Nusa Ceningan. You will find the seaweed farmers all along the coastal roads.

Blue Lagoon

6 *Perilous Beauty Spot*

Make your way by bike to the south west of Nusa Ceningan Island, where you will find the beautiful Blue Lagoon. It may sound like a serene swimming spot, but don't be fooled; although lovely to look at, Blue Lagoon is a wild and treacherous rocky cove with bright blue waves crashing fiercely against limestone walls. There's a cliff edge from which to view this natural beauty spot, but be careful as there are no barriers. Daredevil travellers used to navigate the craggy path around the lagoon to do cliff jumping, although thankfully this activity has since stopped. Blue Lagoon is a magnificent site to simply sit and admire the powerful waves smashing against the shoreline, a striking albeit potentially dangerous situation.

Getting here
From Nusa Lembongan, head south and look for the yellow bridge that links to Nusa Ceningan. Turn right and head along the coastal road. Blue Lagoon is located on the south west of the island.

Secret Beach

7 *Deserted and Rugged Shoreline*

Nestled in a bay on the south of Nusa Ceningan is the often deserted Secret Beach. Like many of the beaches around these islands, the currents are strong and the water unsafe to swim in, but it sure is lovely to look at. There's a narrow strip of biscuit-coloured sand with pieces of driftwood washed up on the shore and a line of thick green shrubs edging behind it. Waves sweep the beach and blast the chunks of rocks embedded into the sand. Dig your bare feet into the soft sand and stand there while the foam-crested waves flow around your legs. Secret Beach is hidden away, so you'll likely be its only visitors. When finding the beach, look out for *Villa Trevally*, which is the small resort next to it. You probably wouldn't want to spend too much time here as there isn't any shade, but it's worth a stop off to admire this beautiful beach.

Getting here
Secret Beach is located on the south west of the island, not far from Blue Lagoon. Look out for *Villa Trevally*, which is the resort next to the beach.

Crystal Bay Beach

8 *Remote Island Life*

A visit to Nusa Penida is much like stepping onto an island that time forgot. The island is best reached by taking a long-armed, wooden outrigger boat from Nusa Lembongan, and the journey takes around 30-40 minutes. The waters at Crystal Bay have become popular with snorkelers and divers attracted to the active underwater world. You can come ashore and step onto its beach, where you will find a distinctly tropical scene. Tall palm trees flank a thin strip of sugary white sand, with colourful boats propped up on the shore. The island is simple, and the locals are friendly. Women spend their mornings washing their clothes in the shallow river, young children splash around and slow cows graze on the green grass. There's a true desert island feel to this place. It is definitely a good half-day trip, with a combination of snorkeling and beach.

Getting here

From Nusa Lembongan, you can organise someone to take you on a boat over to Crystal Bay at Nusa Penida. The journey takes around 30-40 minutes, and the water can be choppy!

LOST GUIDES
LOVES

Boutique Retreat
Sal Secret Spot, Bingin

Eating Experience
Locavore, Ubud

Beach Vibes
Bingin Beach, Bingin

Shopping Spree
Magali Pascal, Seminyak

Evening Entertainment
Sunday at Single Fin, Uluwatu

Swim-up Bar
Potato Head Beach Club, Seminyak

Jungle Hideaway
Alam Ubud, Ubud

Hipster Hangout
Crate Café, Canggu

Indonesian Antiques
Tan Celagi, Mas nr. Ubud

Sunset Scenes
Sandy Bay Beach Club, Nusa Lembongan

My Bali Travel Notes

Date	Location	Notes

Date	Location	Notes

Date	Location	Notes

Date	Location	Notes

Date   Location   Notes

Date	Location	Notes

Date	Location	Notes

Date   Location   Notes

Date	Location	Notes

Acknowledgements

Lost Guides – Bali was proudly crowdfunded by 146 lovely people who helped me to raise $4,790, which went towards the production of the book. (You can check out my crowdfunding page and watch the video on publishizer.com/lost-guides-bali.)

A huge thanks to everyone that contributed towards my crowdfunding goal and helped me to make this book a reality.

Patrons
Alfred Waring, Babak Ghatineh, Ben Ainley, Chris O'Keeffe, Erica Hanson, Flo Bell, Holly O'Keeffe, Jessie Hislop, Oliver Chittenden, Rosamund Chittenden, Sabrina Nguyen, Shahla Ghatineh, William Wright

I couldn't have done this book without my wonderful friends and family who helped me initially with the exploration side of the project. My boyfriend Babak, my Mum, my friend Elly who climbed down cliffs with me looking for beaches, Will and Gen who kindly shared their secret Bali spots with me and for letting me crash at their home too many times, Putu Arnawa who introduced me to the artists hidden away in villages, and many more people who helped me along the way. Thanks to everyone who has given me their advice, shared their knowledge and donated their skills and time to help me to pull this project off. Thanks to my editor Josie for giving me your time and patience and for even working on your honeymoon! I am forever grateful to you all.

Additional photography:

Morning Light Yoga	Desa Seni
Sunset Paradise Villa	Yoga Barn
Sal Secret Spot – Olive Chittenden	Kush
The Cashew Tree	Hubud – Franz Navarrete
Mick's Place	Locavore
Cuca	Room 4 Dessert
Metis	Villa Voyage